MONTGOMERY COLLEGE LIBRARY
GERMANTOWN CAMPUS

Kevin V. Mulcahy
is an assistant professor of political science
at Mills College.

Richard S. Katz
is an assistant professor of political science
at John Hopkins University.

America Votes
What You Should Know About Elections Today

KEVIN V. MULCAHY

RICHARD S. KATZ

Prentice-Hall, Inc., *Englewood Cliffs, New Jersey*

Library of Congress Cataloging in Publication Data

MULCAHY, KEVIN V
 America votes.

 (A Spectrum Book)
 Includes bibliographical references and index.
 1. Elections—United States. 2. Voting—United
States. 3. United States—Politics and government—
1945-   I. Katz, Richard S., joint author.
II. Title.
JK1965.M84   329'.023'73092   76-15592
ISBN 0-13-023796-5
ISBN 0-13-023788-4 pbk.

© 1976 by Prentice-Hall, Inc., Englewood Cliffs, New Jersey

All rights reserved. No part of this book
may be reproduced in any form or by any means
without permission in writing from the publisher.

A Spectrum Book

10 9 8 7 6 5 4 3 2 1

Printed in the United States of America

Prentice-Hall International, Inc., *London*
Prentice-Hall of Australia Pty. Limited, *Sydney*
Prentice-Hall of Canada, Ltd., *Toronto*
Prentice-Hall of India Private Limited, *New Delhi*
Prentice-Hall of Japan, Inc., *Tokyo*
Prentice-Hall of Southeast Asia Pte. Ltd., *Singapore*

in memory of

VINCENT A. MULCAHY

for

MARTHA D. KATZ

Contents

Acknowledgments   vi

CHAPTER ONE

Elections and Voting   1

Why Elections?   3
Voting Today   5
American Elections   8
Who May Vote?   15
Parties and Elections   17
Implications   19

CHAPTER TWO

Voter Turnout — 21

The Psychology of Voting	23
The Sociology of Voting	26
The Electorates Compared	29
Primary Elections	32
Implications	33

CHAPTER THREE

Party Loyalty — 36

The Nature of Party Identification	37
Groups and Party Identification	39
Party Identification and Voting	42
Partisanship and Independents	46
Implications	49

CHAPTER FOUR

Party Competition — 51

The American Party System	52
Competition in the States	54
State Political Behavior	58
Competitiveness and Candidates	61
Competition Within Parties	67
Implications	70

CHAPTER FIVE

Issues and Voters   74

Issue Voting	75
Public Opinions	76
Issues and Party Identification	82
The Rational Voter	84
Implications	86

CHAPTER SIX

Values and Voters   91

Political Socialization	91
American Political Culture	95
The Independent Ethos	104
Implications	107

CHAPTER SEVEN

The Future of Voting   110

Conclusions	110
Speculations	114

Acknowledgments

Every book represents a host of intellectual and editorial debts. We would like to note a few of these.

As teachers, Bernard Hennessey, Madeleine Adler, Elmer Cornwell, Donald Stokes, Philip Converse, and David Mayhew introduced us to the study of electoral behavior and political parties. Professors Ronald M. Schneider and Henry W. Morton, Chairmen of the Queens College Political Science Department, arranged secretarial assistance. Anna Hiller did an exemplary job of typing the manuscript.

Lynne Lumsden and Ron Chambers of Prentice-Hall encouraged this project. Martin Machowsky contributed able research and computational assistance, and Norman Adler made many helpful suggestions in this book's early stages. Judith Katz and Evelyn Stern provided a sustained critical review—both analytic and stylistic.

The data used in this book were made available by the Inter-University Consortium for Political Research. Neither the Consortium nor the individuals acknowledged above bear any responsibility for the analyses or interpretations presented here.

CHAPTER ONE

Elections and Voting

Confidence in elections has hit rock bottom. Revelations of illegal campaign contributions, CREEP's dirty tricks, and the Watergate coverup have been particularly devastating. Such scandals give Tammany Hall's ballot stuffing and the Harding Administration's Teapot Dome an air of pleasant nostalgia. When urged to get politically involved, people reply that politics is a dirty business. When canvassed to vote, people respond that voting only encourages the politicians. No matter how interested people may be in the public good, many accept convicted Nixon aide Gordon Strachan's moral: "Don't get involved in politics!"

The low evaluation of elections reflects a general decline in the standing of political institutions (see Figure 1-1). Trust in elections, parties, and congressmen has fallen sharply among people generally and especially among Blacks. In 1964 the voters were asked, "How much do you feel that having elections makes the government pay attention to what the people think: a good deal, some, or not very much?" The difference between those saying a great deal and those saying not very much was about 58% for Whites and 62% for Blacks. By 1972,

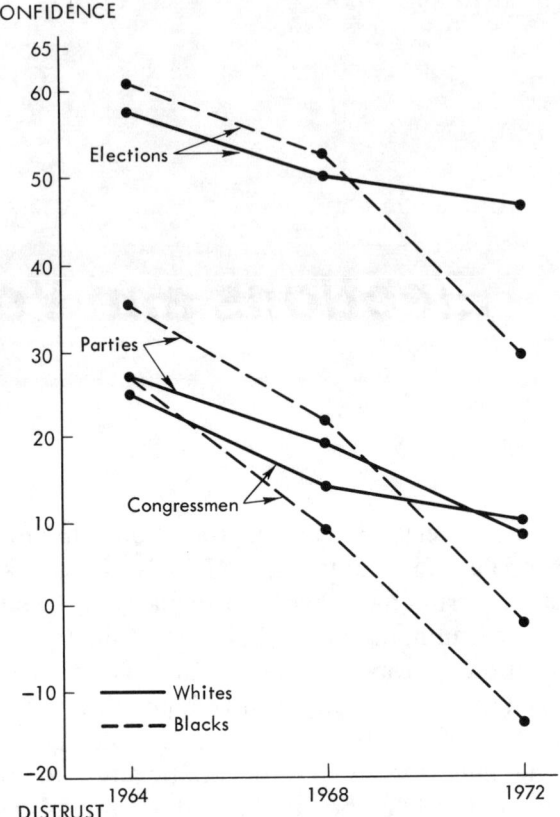

Figure 1-1 Confidence in Leaders, Parties, and Elections, 1964-1972

Source: Arthur H. Miller, "Political Issues and Trust in Government, 1964-1970," American Political Science Review 68 (September 1974), 990.

these figures had fallen to 50% for Whites and under 30% for Blacks. During the same period, similar decreases also occurred in the proportion thinking that parties make the government pay attention to what people think and in the proportion thinking that congressmen pay attention to the people who elect them.[1]

Politics has been pretty traumatic in the past ten years; dissatisfaction with the political system is a logical outcome.

[1] Arthur H. Miller, "Political Issues and Trust in Government: 1964-1970," *American Political Science Review* 68 (September 1974), 951-72, 989-1001.

The failure of the avowed peace candidate in 1964 to end the war (instead Johnson ordered its escalation), the divisiveness of the 1968 campaign (despite Humphrey's politics of joy), and the perceived absence of real alternatives in 1972 (even the AFL-CIO stayed neutral) badly discredited elections. Only 37% of those registered bothered to vote in 1974. With such a disgraceful turnout, we may have to go to the Smithsonian to see *Homo civicus Americanus.* Is the voter a vanishing species?

Voting needs to be re-examined in the light of this electoral truancy. To assume that everyone should vote, while berating those who do not, begs the question. Why are so many Americans indifferent to what the civics books call the precious gift of representative government? Why don't more of us (indeed, all who are eligible) exercise the franchise? If these rights are so important, yet people remain so indifferent to them, what are the political implications? If the vast majority of the American people do not seem to care about voting, why should you?

WHY ELECTIONS?

Criticizing elections is a national pastime. People denounce elections as unrepresentative, unedifying, and unreliable. Are these criticisms valid? Before answering, we must first know what elections are supposed to do. Why do we have elections?

In the most elementary sense, elections are devices for picking people to fill public offices. Where more than one person wants a given office, elections allow the public to sort the contenders out. Popular election legitimizes a democratic government where the right to rule is not by divine sanction but by the will *of the people.* Voting stamps popular approval upon a government. Whatever we might think of elected officials, those with majority support can rightfully speak *for the people.* In a democracy, sovereignty is exercised not by a person or party, but *by the people.*

Periodic competitive elections establish popular control over government policies and over those holding public office. Even officials who exercise independent judgment must be sensitive to public opinion if they wish to be re-elected. No official, however popular or powerful, can ignore constituency interests indefinitely. The need to secure a popular mandate gives the public some control over policy formulation. At the minimum, the voters can throw the rascals out.

Elections provide a measure of participation in the management of public affairs. Equally important, they contribute to an individual's personal development. "Leaving things to the Government, like leaving them to Providence, is synonymous with caring nothing about them, and accepting their results, when disagreeable, as visitations of Nature."[2] Debating public issues, making a decision, and acting on that decision in the polling booth improve a person's self-worth. The voters can gain a heightened sense of importance through participation in making decisions that affect their destinies. Free elections, especially where issues are fully debated, help create an active, thinking, and informed citizenry. Whatever the outcome, electoral participation furthers an individual's self-actualization.

Deciding to participate, however, is an act quite aside from arguments that every vote counts in determining election results. One has a better chance of being killed on the way to the polls than one has of actually affecting the outcome of a contest.[3] People vote for personal reasons: psychic satisfaction, party loyalty, civic duty. We vote out of a sense of subjectively felt responsibility or obligation.[4] Unlike certain democratic nations (Australia and Switzerland, for example), there are no sanctions imposed for nonparticipation. When we forsake an evening's television or brave the rain to vote, we do so because we want to

---

[2] John Stuart Mill, *Considerations on Representative Government* (Chicago: Henry Regnery Company, 1962), p. 52.

[3] B. F. Skinner, *Walden II* (New York: Macmillan, 1948), 265.

[4] See Gabriel A. Almond and Sidney Verba, *The Civic Culture* (Boston: Little, Brown and Company, 1965); and R. E. Gooden and K. W. S. Roberts, "The Ethical Voter," *American Political Science Review* 69 (September 1975), 926–28.

or because we feel that we ought to. Low voter turnout points to a decline in our standards of citizenship.

VOTING TODAY

Despite their importance for democratic government, elections are in increasing trouble. While turnout in presidential elections once averaged about 80% in the latter half of the nineteenth century, the 64% reached in 1960 was considered noteworthy. Since then, turnout has reached new lows. At the same time, nonelectoral protest has surged: protest marches, campus turmoil, police riots, terrorist bombings. Apparently, many people judge voting less effective for exerting pressure than direct action.[5] Little wonder that public confidence in the political process has plummeted.

The rising public cynicism and declining trust in government is shown in Table 1-1. The percentage of the voters expressing distrust that the government in Washington would do the right thing doubled from 1964 to 1972. In the same period, public cynicism—expressed as belief in government's domination by a few big interests—rose from 29% to about 50%. Watergate and the Vietnam War certainly contributed to a disbelief in governmental trustworthiness and representativeness. Some of these attitudes could indicate a healthy scepticism and a traditional American distrust of government. But too often, they represent a thoroughgoing rejection of positive political action that threatens to undermine democracy's mass base.

Democratic government rests upon public support and involvement. Politics is a bully forum in which to educate the people. Campaigns, however, have rarely lived up to this ideal. Less and less attention is devoted to public debate of the issues in American electoral campaigns. Instead, images constructed

---

[5] See Michael Lipsky, "Protest as a Political Resource," *American Political Science Review* 62 (December 1968), 1144-58.

Table 1-1 Trust in Government is Decreasing and Political Cynicism is Increasing.

How much of the time do you think you can trust the government in Washington to do what is right—just about always, most of the time, or only some of the time?

	1964	1966	1968	1970
Always	14.0%	17.0%	7.5%	6.4%
Most of the Time	62.0	48.0	53.4	47.1
Only Some of the Time[a]	22.0	31.0	37.0	44.2
Don't Know	2.0	4.0[b]	2.1	2.3
Total	100.0%	100.0%	100.0%	100.0%

Would you say the government is pretty much run by a few big interests looking out for themselves or that it is run for the benefit of all the people?

	1964	1966	1968	1970
For Benefit of All	64.0%	53.0%	51.8%	40.6%
Few Big Interests[a]	29.0	34.0	39.2	49.6
Other; Depends; Both Checked	4.0	6.0	4.6	5.0
Don't Know	3.0	7.0	4.3	4.8
Total	100.0%	100.0%	100.0%	100.0%

[a]Indicates responses interpreted as "cynical."
[b]Includes 1% coded "It depends."

Source: Miller, "Political Issues and Trust in Government," 953.

by political marketing firms dominate the campaign. Pictures of candidates surrounded by children and dogs may be heart warming, but they reveal little about their policies. Appeals to the voter's worst instincts may be successful, but they destroy fair play. Vacuous promises may gain votes, but they do not further responsible government. The low road in political campaigning is not only reprehensible—it defrauds the public.

Electoral corruption, while different from the nineteenth century variety, is pervasive. Dirty tricks like cancelling the hall rented for an opponent's rally or bribing a railway engineer to pull the train from the platform while a candidate is speaking may seem like innocent pranks. Yet too frequently these escalate into all-out war on the opposition and pranks become felonies. Knowing receipt of illegal campaign contributions and the laundering of illegal money destroy the legitimacy of elections and public confidence in elected officials. Influence peddling and bribery by elected officials diminish public trust in the electoral process for choosing high quality leaders. Elections can only legitimize government if fundamental fairness is observed and if public office is treated as a public trust.

In classical Athenian democracy officials were chosen by lot rather than by election. Athenian democracy did not need elections because Athens was small enough for individual participation. Although every Athenian citizen could expect to hold a major public office at some time in his life, in mass societies like ours, this is not possible. Elections are necessary to give the average citizen, with little hope of holding office, a voice in political decision making. If modern citizens can rarely make decisions themselves, they can at least decide who will do the deciding for them. Free elections provide the opportunity for choice. To contest elections freely requires the right to debate political issues freely. Freedom of speech and the press, as well as free association and assembly for those who oppose the government of the day, are essential to meaningful elections. Free elections thus entail the basic protection of the Bill of Rights.[6]

The right to decide who will hold public office indirectly confers the power to decide public policy. Candidates stand for election on platforms built with electoral promises. When voters select candidates, they select policies as well. Fear of a retalia-

---

[6]See W. J. M. Mackenzie, *Free Elections* (London: George Allen and Unwin, 1958).

tory electorate forces politicians to honor their pledges. While not free to make policy, voters may choose among a limited number of platforms. Voting transcends personalities as candidates compete to offer more thoughtful policy proposals. In free elections, the voters may impose limits on government officials beyond which they stray only at the risk of defeat.

Elections have a special place in American history. "No taxation without representation," the battle cry of the American Revolution, asserts that laws are valid only when made by elected representatives. The 1860 election results triggered the Civil War. The Southern states announced that they would secede from the Union if Abraham Lincoln were elected President; he was and they did. Many of the major controversies of the 1960s and 1970s—civil rights acts, legislative reapportionment, presidential candidate selection—are disputes about the conduct of elections. Where British history is punctuated by the death of kings and French history by new constitutions, presidential elections are the watersheds of American political life.

AMERICAN ELECTIONS

Americans elect more officials more frequently than any other people. At the national level, we choose a president and get a vice-president. At the state level we vote for a wide variety of offices: a governor, two United States Senators and maybe a lieutenant governor, attorney general, secretary of state, and treasurer. We may also elect an assortment of more exotic officers, such as a commissioner of charities and a custodian of voting machines. Within each state we also elect state legislators and city councilmen, county executives and mayors, school board members, district attorneys, and perhaps judges as well as sheriffs, coroners, and canine control officers. And if this array is not sufficiently bewildering, remember that candidates for these offices are often chosen by intra-party elections (primaries).

General elections fall on the first Tuesday after the first Monday in November. Presidential elections occur every four years in the years divisible by four (1976, 1980). In even-numbered years, the entire House of Representatives and one-third of the Senate are elected. Statewide officials and state legislators are typically elected in non-presidential even-numbderd years (1974, 1978); local elections are usually scheduled in the odd-numbered years. The frequency and timing of elections specifically depends upon length of term and upon other peculiarities. Many specialized elections (like those for school boards) and all primaries are held at times other than November. Many states also allow questions to be put to the voters at general elections. These referenda, propositions, bond proposals, and constitutional amendments ask the voters to decide "yes" or "no" on particular issues of public policy. Assuming one can keep track of all these electoral opportunities, an average American could vote in two or three elections yearly, choosing over thirty candidates and answering as many as twenty questions.

Election rules and procedures vary widely. Nonetheless, the predominant electoral system in the United States is "single-member, plurality election." To elect the state legislature, for example, the state is divided up into districts from which one member is chosen. At the election, voters get a ballot listing the candidates in their district. Each voter may select one candidate; and the one with the most votes wins, regardless of how many votes were cast for other candidates. A plurality (one more than the next contender) suffices for election, not a majority (50% plus 1 of the votes cast). Governors and U.S. Senators are also elected by this system; each state is, then, one single-member district.

The presidential electoral system is a special case of single-member plurality election. The president is formally elected by the Electoral College, not by popular vote. Each state has electoral votes equal to its number of senators and congressmen. (California has the most electoral votes with forty-five; the fewest a state can have is three. The District of Columbia also has three electoral votes.) Each state party proposes a slate of electors pledged to its presidential candidate. The election in November is really between these slates of electors, even though their names do not appear on the ballot. The slate with the most votes statewide wins all the electoral votes; and these are later cast as pledged. However, there is no legal requirement that electors must vote as pledged; occasionally one will not. Second, the slates of electors need not support the nominee of their national party. In 1948, for example, there were no electors pledged to Truman on the ballot in the Southern states. Within the Electoral College, a majority (not just a plurality) is required. If no candidate has at least 50% of the electoral votes, the outcome is decided in the House of Representatives with each state casting one vote according to the majority decision of its congressmen. It is quite possible for a candidate with a slim popular plurality to receive a landslide in the Electoral College. Indeed, it is possible for the candidate with fewer popular votes to win a majority in the Electoral College: Such was the case when Benjamin Harrison won over Grover Cleveland in 1888. (A special electoral commission settled the disputed 1876 election for Hayes, although Tilden probably had more votes.)

Luckily the Electoral College system has produced few such affronts to popular choice. Minority presidents, however, have been common: Richard Nixon in 1968, John Kennedy in 1960, Harry Truman in 1948, Woodrow Wilson in 1912, Abraham Lincoln in 1860. In each case, third parties made strong showings in the popular, although not in the Electoral College, vote. The House of Representatives chose two presidents in the nineteenth century: Thomas Jefferson in 1804 (an electoral fluke rectified by the Twelfth Amendment), and John Quincy Adams in 1824 (an election Andrew Jackson claimed was stolen). Still, third party candidates, like George Wallace, periodically threaten to throw the election into the House of Representatives, where the voting system blatantly ignores population differences as well as the popular vote. If this were to happen, the way would be open for the worst kind of political deals. Voter confidence would be shaken, and if the House elected anyone but the candidate with a popular plurality, a Constitutional crisis would result.

Like almost all political arrangements, the single-member plurality system is not neutral; some groups are advantaged and others are disadvantaged. In particular, the large, established parties are favored over the small and nascent parties. This system also encourages two-party, rather than multi-party, competition.[7] Because the winner takes all in each district, third parties will have little to show for their efforts unless their strength is highly concentrated. The difference between the number of legislative seats won by a party and its proportion of the vote is often great. The winning party tends to be over-represented in the legislature.[8] Even in multi-party New York, the Liberals and Conservatives are more likely to endorse the candidate of one or the other major party rather than to run a candidate of their own. It does a party no good to do very well in the voting if it consistently fails to get a plurality. "Winning isn't the most important thing; it's the only thing" is even truer in politics than in football.

The fact that winning requires only a plurality creates not only the possibility of minority victors but of electoral spoilers. Some parties and their candidates are far too weak to elect anyone themselves; but they are strong enough to deny victory to the party that would ordinarily win. Their goal can be issue education and consciousness raising; it is more often political

[7] See Maurice Duverger, *Political Parties* (New York: John Wiley and Sons, 1959), pp. 216-225; and Douglas W. Rae, *The Political Consequences of Electoral Laws,* 2nd ed. (New Haven: Yale University Press, 1971), Chapter 10. Rae points out that the discrimination against small parties, and hence against multi-party competition, applies only at the level of individual constituencies.

[8] See Edward R. Tufte, "The Relationship Between Seats and Votes in Two-Party Systems," *American Political Science Review* 67 (June 1973), 540-54.

blackmail. This tactic can force a major party into policies that it would not otherwise support: as, for example, was attempted by the Dixiecrats in 1948 and by George Wallace in 1968. While American parties are not known for either organizational or ideological coherence, the consequences of splintering and of splinter parties in the single-member, national-district presidential election help to keep them together.

Because elections are decided on a district by district basis, how these district lines are drawn is crucial. Unless districts have equal populations, any claim to the equality of each vote is fraudulent. The Supreme Court recognized the principle of one person, one vote, in *Baker* v. *Carr* (1962) and in *Reynolds* v. *Sims* (1964)—taken together these decisions (along with several others) held that constituencies for virtually every legislative body in the country (except the United States Senate) must be of roughly equal population.[9]

Yet ensuring districts that are of equal population size does not in itself guarantee fairness. It is possible—theoretically—for a party to win 26% of the popular vote and get 51% of the legislative seats if it polls just over half the votes in just half the districts. Although the likelihood of such an electoral outcome is remote, it is nevertheless possible for a party that controls the state legislature to draw district boundaries in order to maximize its electoral advantage. Flagrantly drawing district boundaries to suit the majority party is termed gerrymandering, a term that honors Governor Elbridge Gerry of Massachusetts who, in 1812, signed (although he disapproved of) a bill carving out a district shaped like a salamander. Of course, not all odd-shaped districts are the result of gerrymanders; equivalent results can be produced by different means. Still, some strange configurations remain—like the California congressional district that was contiguous only at low tide, and the New York legislative district connected by running down the middle of a street including the street but not the buildings on either side.

[9] See Carl A. Auerbach, "The Reapportionment Cases: One Person, One Vote—One Vote, One Value," *1964 Supreme Court Review* 1, 68–70.

Sometimes gerrymanders are used not to favor the majority party but to discriminate against a particular group—most frequently Blacks. Dividing a group among several districts dilutes its strength and diminishes the probability of electing one of its own. The most blatant racial gerrymanders have been ruled unconstitutional: Witness the 1957 attempt to redraw Tuskegee, Alabama from a square to a "28 sided sea horse" that excluded all but five Blacks from the city limits without affecting a single White. Yet proving that a gerrymander has occurred is difficult;[10] moreover, one group's gerrymander may be another's equal representation, thus raising the difficult theoretical question of whether every ascriptive group is entitled to its own legislative district represented by a member of that group. But theory aside, the ethnographic politics involved in such districting would surely exacerbate ethnic and racial tensions. Since each group would probably attempt to maximize its particularistic appeals in order to insure greater political representation, the consequences for building inter-group electoral coalitions and maintaining legislative party cohesion would be severely negative.

Exceptions to the single-member plurality scheme do exist, but they are rare. Many Southern states require majority election; if no candidate has 50% of the vote (a possibility when there are more than two candidates), a run-off election between the top two contenders occurs. This procedure was especially effective in preventing Blacks from winning when the White vote was split; all the White votes could coalesce on the second ballot. Cambridge, Massachusetts elects its city council with a single-transferable ballot by which voters rank all the candidates in the order of their choice. Multi-member plurality elections choose many other city councils: Each voter chooses one candidate, but the top five or ten are elected rather than only the top one. Illinois uses a cumulative voting system to elect its House of Representatives. Each person has two votes and three repre-

---

[10]Frank Sorauf, *Party and Representation* (New York: Atherton Press, 1963), pp. 21–31.

sentatives are elected from each district. Since minority party supporters may give both their votes to one candidate, they are generally able to elect one of the three representatives.

The winner-take-all provision of the American electoral system has particularly affected presidential campaign strategy. It enhances the importance of the large industrial states such as California, New York, Pennsylvania, Illinois, Ohio, Texas, and Michigan, which account for 211 of the 538 electoral votes. A candidate need win in only these seven states plus a few here and there in order to win the presidency. Small states, especially if aligned with the opposition, can be safely ignored. And since it would be politically futile to visit every state, a candidate's limited resources (both time and money) are better spent in states with large blocs of electoral votes.

Since each of these states is also highly competitive, concentrated urban minorities can play a pivotal role in swinging an election to a particular candidate. The winner-take-all provision for state electoral votes disenfranchises opposition party supporters; they might do better if the electoral votes were allocated proportionately to the popular vote. On the other hand, the provision does compensate for the over-representation of nonurban areas in other parts of the political system and it also gives minorities what little political leverage they possess. Direct election of the president would not be a neutral procedural reform; it would profoundly affect party organization, group representation, political appeals, and the distribution of power.[11] Electoral College reform is a special case of the general rule that procedural changes involve substantive changes.

Even ballot form is not completely neutral. Since the introduction of the Australian ballot in Massachusetts in 1888, all states have government operated secret balloting. Ballot layout, however, is not uniform. One-third of the states use the office

[11]See Wallace S. Sayre and Judith H. Parris, *Voting for President: The Electoral College and the American Political System* (Washington: The Brookings Institution, 1970).

block format: Candidates for each office are grouped together. Party designations are provided, but there is no way to cast a straight ticket except by voting for each office separately. The rest of the states have a party column format: Candidates' names are laid out in a grid arrangement with office defining the rows and party the columns (or conversely). This lists all the candidates of a single party together. Provision is generally made for a straight party ballot to be cast by marking a single "x" or by pulling a single lever at the head of the party column.

The party column ballot encourages straight ticket voting; the office block form enhances the importance of individual candidates. Party column ballots encourage people to vote for all the offices being contested. The office block ballot helps candidates with well-known names or a strong personal campaign organization.

WHO MAY VOTE?

The Constitution says very little about the right to vote; determining eligibility was left to the states. Article I, Section 2 only required that those eligible to vote "for the most numerous Branch of a State Legislature" be allowed to vote in House of Representatives elections. In 1789, about one in thirty adults could vote. Women and slaves were disenfranchised; many states had property qualifications. In New York, only those owning land worth at least £40 could vote. In Virginia, the qualification was ownership of 100 unsettled acres, twenty-five acres with a house and plantation, or freehold of any house or lot in a city or town. While Vermont abolished property qualifications in the 1820s, the property qualification in Virginia was in force until 1850.

The Fifteenth Amendment in 1870 was the first substantial federal intervention into the question of voter qualifications. It required that "The right of citizens of the United States to vote shall not be denied or abridged by the United States or by any State on account of race, color, or previous condition of servitude." The South largely circumvented this measure, however, through the "White Primary," discriminatory literacy tests, and the poll tax. The first assumed that primaries were private elections not covered by the Fifteenth Amendment, even though Democratic primary victory was tantamount to election. *Smith* v. *Allwright* ruled the White Primary unconstitutional in 1944. While literacy tests still exist, the Voting Rights Act of 1965 largely prevents racial discrimination in their application. The Twenty-Fourth Amendment to the Constitution outlawed the poll tax.

Women were the next group to be enfranchised. The states took the initiative when Wyoming (then a territory) first allowed women to vote on an equal footing with men in 1869. Earlier, some states had allowed certain women to vote in some elections. (Widows and unmarried women meeting the property qualification could vote in school elections in Kentucky in 1838.) By 1914, eleven states (all west of the Mississippi) had enfranchised women. After an intensive campaign during World War I, the suffragettes won ratification, in 1920, of the Nineteenth Amendment, giving women full voting equality in all elections. The Twenty-Sixth Amendment lowered the voting age to eighteen and represents the most recent suffrage expansion.

The Supreme Court has increasingly come to view suffrage as a right of citizenship which is therefore subject to federal control. Consequently, literacy tests (where required) must be offered in both Spanish and English; and if a substantial Spanish speaking population exists the ballot must be bilingual. Residency requirements are also limited: Living in the same place for thirty days is legally sufficient. Nevertheless, inmates of asylums and prisons cannot vote; neither can some ex-offenders.

Voter registration is the great disenfranchiser of Americans today. In order to vote, one must not only be qualified but registered. Personal registration was introduced in order to combat corrupt machine practices like the Tammany Hall advice to "Vote early and often." A Denver man testified to having voted 125 times in one election; he quit when the organization lowered the price of a vote from one dollar to fifty cents. Buying votes with bottles of whiskey was common practice in rural Pennsylvania even after World War II.

Personal registration has corrected such flagrant abuses, but the electorate has been diminished. While the requirements are simple, they must be fulfilled in person at specific times in advance of the election. In many states, registration must be periodically renewed. Compliance is solely an individual responsibility; and ignorance, forgetfulness, and laziness take a large toll, especially among the poor. As many as 27% of the potential electorate may be disenfranchised because of their failure to register.[12]

PARTIES AND ELECTIONS

Mass suffrage made modern political parties necessary. Before mass voting (both in the United States and in Europe), there had been fairly stable legislative groupings but no rank-and-file organizations. Members knew the people upon whom their re-election depended and would deal with them on a personal basis. But as more people became eligible to vote, constituency organizations were required to whip up the party faithful, to drive the less motivated to the polls, and to finance and staff campaigns. American parties were created and are maintained to fight elections. And at the same time, parties play a decisive role in running elections. In order to understand the political process, one must recognize that elections and parties are tied together in mutual dependence.

Parties do the things that make elections practically possible. Elections require candidates; the parties supply them. Party

[12]See Stanley Kelly, Jr., Richard E. Ayers, and William C. Bowen, "Registration and Voting: Putting First Things First," *American Political Science Review* 61 (June 1967), 359–79.

conventions select presidential and vice-presidential candidates in accordance with party rules. State-run primary elections select most other candidates; and these are also a party affair. Nomination for office is usually a reward for faithful party service. Mass elections require people to lick envelopes, ring door bells, schedule speeches, watch the polls, and get out the vote. The parties raise the thousands of workers and millions of dollars needed for an effective national campaign. Parties frame election issues. The party conventions write the campaign platforms that shape government policy. The party label links candidates to each other, to the party nationally, and to the electoral process. Party provides an element of organizational and historical continuity from one election to the next. In this way, the whole party must accept responsibility for the actions of its members in office.

American parties are fundamentally opportunist; they are first of all interested in winning elections. Consequently, parties adopt policies they expect to be popular. Both parties attempt to maximize their share of the votes by seeking the middle of the political spectrum. Hence the parties are both moderate and similar to each other. To be ideologically extreme is to invite electoral repudiation.[13] In fact, there is tension within the parties. The professionals, for whom winning is overwhelmingly important, seek to maximize votes and let tactical considerations dictate policy stands. For the amateurs—the volunteers who are a party's grass roots strength—procedure and policy are paramount. They would rather be right than be president or assemblyman.[14] Unchecked, amateurism might force the party into extreme positions. On the other hand, amateurs are a party's conscience; and they keep professionals policy-honest. The tension between, say, the George McGovern and Richard Daly or Barry Goldwater and Rogers Morton

[13]See Anthony Downs, *An Economic Theory of Democracy* (New York: Harper & Row, 1957), pp. 51–74.
[14]Joseph A. Schlesinger, "The Primary Goals of Political Parties: A Clarification of Positive Theory," *American Political Science Review* 69 (September 1975), 840–49.

wings of a party can be healthy if it is marked by mutual respect and fair play. Too often, however, this tension degenerates into especially vicious domestic quarreling that obscures their mutual dependence. A balance between professionals and amateurs insures parties that are not only moderate but sufficiently different on policy matters, thus giving the public a real choice at the polls.

IMPLICATIONS

Declining satisfaction with the electoral process, the disintegration of traditional party organizations, and increased talk of reform force us to reassess American elections. How do voters make up their minds? What is the role of parties in an election? How do reforms affect the quality of the electoral process? Most important, do elections need reform and what might be its consequences?

An election is extremely complex, full of ramifications, and influenced by a wide variety of forces. Reforms to broaden participation have implications both for the parties and for responsible government. Broadening the scope of electoral decision making may make excessive demands on voters and narrow the range of citizens actually participating. And if this new and smaller electorate is seriously unrepresentative of the total citizenry, the reformed system may be worse than the original.

Elections come in all kinds. Turnout rates alone demonstrate the wide differences between presidential general elections and congressional primaries. To understand American politics, one must distinguish among the compositions and behaviors of the electorates at different levels, for different offices, and at different times. This book seeks to explain these differences.

These comparisons will put electoral reform in perspective. What is the relationship between the electorate's quantity and its quality? What effect does party organization, party identification, and party competition have on voting? Is each vote unique or is it rooted in our historical and cultural background?

Answers raise two paradoxes surrounding American elections. The first is a paradox of participation: the higher the turnout rate, the lower the electorate's level of interest, information, and discrimination. The smaller electorate, although higher in quality, is unrepresentative of the interests and aspirations of those less likely to vote. The second paradox is one of democracy. Increased popular control over the parties and over individual politicians seems desirable. Yet by weakening the accountability and responsibility of the party as a governing coalition, it makes popular control over policy more difficult. Throughout this book we consider the practical implications of these paradoxes and of the differences between state and national elections.

Where are American elections going? What is the future of voting? What are the long-run consequences of the many reforms in campaign practice and election rules? If elections really decide America's future, and if voting is the most important act of a democratic citizen, we should try to explain, and, perhaps, to understand these problems.

CHAPTER TWO

Voter Turnout

Voting is the most elementary political act of the democratic citizen. The virtue of voting is emphasized in our schools and re-emphasized by politicians and by the mass media at every election. Almost everyone recognizes an obligation to vote. Yet low turnout is a fact of American political life in even the most exciting elections. Turnout is low compared to the democratic ideal of 100% participation, low compared to the proportion of people who think they should vote, and low compared to the turnout in other democratic countries.

Turnout in Presidential elections averaged 60.5% over the period 1956–1972. This turnout is markedly higher than the level of popular participation in choosing members of the House of Representatives. A comparison of turnout levels for these two types of elections is made in Figure 2-1. Turnout in non-presidential years varies considerably among the states. The average turnout in gubernatorial and senatorial elections in the non-presidential years from 1950 to 1960 was 45.3%. This ranged from Mississippi's low of 4.2% to Idaho's high of

22 *America Votes*

Figure 2-1 Voting Turnout For President and United States House of Representatives, 1952-1974

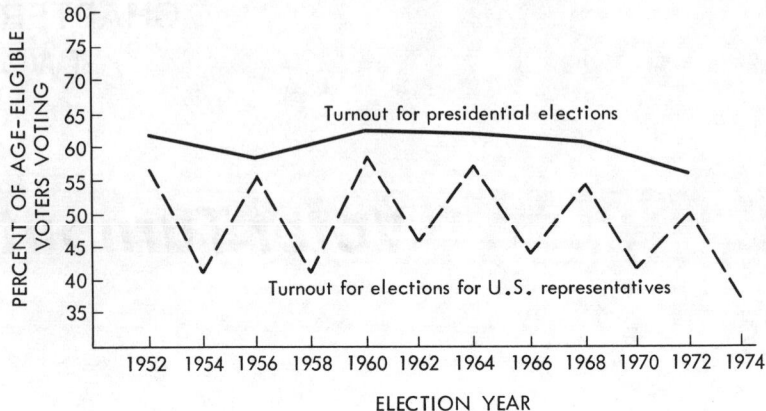

Source: Hugh A. Bone and Austin Ranney. Politics and Voters *(New York: McGraw-Hill, 1976), p. 35.*

64.6%.[1] The rate of voting for local offices is even lower. Ten per cent turnout in an election for mayor or school board, if held in an odd-numbered year, is heavy. The voters' greater interest in national rather than state or local affairs is clear.[2]

The fact that subnational elections have a decidedly lower turnout than national elections is not completely informative.[3] We cannot assume that the subnational electorate exactly reflects the characteristics of the national electorate. A systematic comparison of the two electorates—presidential (national) and non-presidential (subnational)—is necessary. Who votes in

[1] Lester W. Milbrath, "Individuals in Government," in *Politics in the American States: A Comparative Analysis,* 2nd ed., eds. Herbert Jacob and Kenneth N. Vines (Boston: Little Brown, 1971), p. 36.

[2] See M. Kent Jennings and Harmon Ziegler, "The Salience of American State Politics," *American Political Science Review* 64 (June 1970), 523-35.

[3] While fewer people vote in state than in presidential elections, the subnational electorate is substantially a subset of the national—not different people. Over 95% of those voting in 1970 reported voting in 1968; 70% of those who did not vote in 1968 also did not vote in 1970.

state, as distinct from national, elections? Do state voters share identical characteristics with national voters or do they have different social and political traits? What is distinctive about the two electorates?

THE PSYCHOLOGY OF VOTING

An individual's psychological involvement in the election is an important correlate of electoral activity.[4] As Table 2-1 shows, interested people are more likely to vote, albeit at lower levels in state elections. The effect of interest, however, is greater for the subnational electorate where the drama associated with the presidential contest is absent. This is indicated by the sharper fall-off in state turnout with each decrease in interest (21% and 24% respectively) compared to the more modest initial declines in presidential turnout (10% and 25%).

Table 2-1 Interest and Voter Turnout

Degree of Interest	Turnout Subnational 1970	Turnout National 1972
High	77%	86%
Medium	56%	76%
Low	32%	51%

The interested person is the most likely to vote, especially in characteristically low visibility state elections. When interest declines, state turnout plummets. Presidential turnout stays high even among those with only medium interest in the campaign. The highly publicized fireworks of the presidential

[4]Angus Campbell, Philip E. Converse, Warren E. Miller, and Donald E. Stokes, *The American Voter* (New York: John Wiley and Sons, 1960), Chapter 5.

campaign propels to the polls people who otherwise would not vote.

A person's self-assessed competence also affects political participation generally and voting turnout in particular. This sense of efficacy or political effectiveness is measured by responses to questions involving one's assessment of political potency, trust in public officials, and understanding of political matters.[5] The higher the sense of efficacy, the greater the turnout in both electorates, as Table 2-2 illustrates. Of course, at each level of efficacy, turnout is lower in the subnational electorate than in the national.

Table 2-2   Level of Political Efficacy and Likelihood of Voting

Level of Political Efficacy	Turnout Subnational 1970	National 1972
High	71%	88%
	64%	83%
	59%	77%
	54%	66%
Low	46%	59%

Strong attachment to a political party provides the psychological involvement that motivates people to become politically active. People with a strong attachment participate more than those whose attachment is not very strong, those who are leaning toward a party, or those who have no attachment at all. The higher turnout levels associated with more intense partisan feelings are shown in Table 2-3. Just as with interest in the campaign, the impact of declining partisanship is felt more immediately in the subnational electorate. More "not very strong" and "leaning" partisans vote in presidential elections

[5]For the specific questions used in constructing this index of political efficacy, see Angus Campbell, Gerald Gurin, and Warren E. Miller, *The Voter Decides* (Evanston, Ill.: Row, Peterson, 1954), pp. 187-99.

Table 2-3 Partisanship and Likelihood of Voting

Strength of Party Identification	Turnout Subnational 1970	Turnout National 1972
Strong	69%	83%
Not Very Strong	57%	74%
Leaning	52%	74%
Independent	45%	53%

than in state contests. The peculiar nature of the presidential campaign produces a higher but less intensely partisan turnout.

People without a specific party affiliation—the self-conscious Independents—have the lowest turnout. This is particularly evident in state elections where there is no presidential charisma to generate the interest that encourages participation by the nonpartisans. Republicans turn out more than Democrats who turn out more than Independents. These data are shown in Table 2-4.

Table 2-4 Likelihood of Voting by Political Party Preference

Party Preference	Turnout Subnational 1970	Turnout National 1972
Democratic	58%	74%
Independent	49%	66%
Republican	69%	83%

Within each group, those who proclaim no partisan attachment depress the turnout rates. Any partisan attachment, however ill formed, increases the likelihood that the person will participate. This runs counter to the notion of highly motivated and politically active Independents weighing the merits of candidates and issues in their electoral choice. While some do approximate the ideal, the typical Independent proves a normative disappointment.

THE SOCIOLOGY OF VOTING

Socioeconomic status or SES—income, occupation, and education—strongly influences voting.[6] For example, Republicans are generally from higher social strata than either Democrats or Independents. Since their turnout rates are higher, they have an impact on electoral outcomes out of proportion to their numbers. The poor turn out the least and so have less influence than their numbers would dictate.

Table 2-5 presents voter turnout data for several of the SES indicators in presidential and state elections. One basic relation-

Table 2-5 Socioeconomic Status and Likelihood of Voting

Socioeconomic Status	Turnout Subnational 1970	National 1972
Subjective Social Class		
Working	50%	68%
Middle	66%	79%
Educational Level		
Grammar School	47%	58%
High School	54%	70%
College	74%	86%
Post-College	83%	93%
Occupation		
Unskilled	48%	64%
Skilled or Semi-Skilled	59%	77%
White-Collar	64%	78%
Professional and Managerial	69%	85%
Income		
$0 – $5,000	46%	60%
$5,000 – $10,000	54%	68%
$10,000 – $15,000	67%	79%
Over $15,000	76%	89%

[6]Paul F. Lazarsfeld, Bernard Berelson, and Hazel Gaudet, *The People's Choice* (New York: Duell, Sloane, and Pearce, 1944), Chapter 5.

ship stands out: As the level of social status rises, turnout increases. The better educated, with more prestigious occupations and higher incomes, are more likely to vote. For that matter, people who consider themselves middle-class, whether accurately or not, are more likely to vote than those who consider themselves working-class.

Although social class cannot by itself determine political participation or its partisan direction, it does create different life opportunities. Well-paid, college-educated professionals have the resources to gather and evaluate political information. With more at stake, they are more concerned about the outcomes. They are also more likely to be imbued with a middle-class ethic of voting as a civic duty. These are all inducements for high levels of participation in general and for voting participation in particular.

The working-class people have fewer advantages (education, verbal skills, interpersonal competence) in gathering political information, voicing concern, and correctly devising electoral strategies. They are more likely to come from an environment where formal procedures such as voting are little valued. Nor is it likely that they will have perceived a direct connection between elections and the possibility of economic betterment. Yet working-class voters are neither apolitical nor necessarily acquiescent. They gave vocal support to both Robert Kennedy and George Wallace, as well as to Franklin Roosevelt and Huey Long. All appealed to the working man and to working-class aspirations.

Certain groups in the population turn out more than others. Men vote more frequently than women, Whites more than nonwhites, Catholics more than Protestants, and Jews more than either one. Turnout increases up through middle age and then begins to level off.[7] These data are shown in Table 2-6.

Age differences are particularly striking. In presidential elections, voting turnout is at its lowest levels among the young and the old, but for different reasons. While 62% of the twenty-

---

[7]Angus Campbell and Robert L. Kahn, *The People Elect a President* (Ann Arbor, Michigan: Institute for Social Research, 1952), p. 38.

Table 2-6 Turnout Variations: Demographic Groups

Demographic Group	Turnout Subnational 1970	Turnout National 1972
Sex		
Male	59%	76%
Female	56%	70%
Race		
White	59%	73%
Nonwhite	45%	64%
Religion		
Protestant	56%	71%
Catholic	64%	79%
Jewish	74%	91%
Age		
21-29	41%	62%
30-44	59%	76%
45-65	65%	79%
Over 65	61%	68%

one through twenty-nine age group voted in the 1972 presidential election, compared to 68% of those over sixty-five; only 41% of the youngest group turned out in the 1970 state elections, compared to 61% of the oldest group. (In fact, the over sixty-five age group showed a greater turnout than those between ages thirty to forty-four.) There was a 21% difference between voting in national and subnational elections for the youngest group, but only a 7% difference for the oldest. What does this mean?

Voting stability increases as one ages: The old vote in both state and presidential elections or not at all. For the older citizens, participation (or nonparticipation) has become a deeply ingrained habit embracing all elections. The young, however, are not deeply committed to the electoral process.

Election type is important. Young voters may have been mesmerized by the long-standing "selling of the president" syndrome. The excitement engendered by the national campaign has reached the point where subnational contests pale in comparison. Voter turnout depends on campaign stimulation. One votes not out of a sense of duty or of partisan loyalty but because one is aroused. The turnout exhibited by the youngest voters is capricious; they vote when titillated.

THE ELECTORATES COMPARED

Differences between group turnout levels in the national and subnational electorates mean that the electorates have different overall compositions. The subnational electorate has a greater proportion of people who express high interest in political campaigns and a somewhat greater proportion of people who evaluate their political effectiveness highly. The subnational electorate is also stronger in its partisan attachments. Independents are a smaller percentage of the subnational voting population than of the national.

The subnational electorate has higher social status than the national. It is composed of proportionately more people who think of themselves as middle-class, who work at prestigious jobs, and who are economically well off. The subnational voters are generally less well educated, but this is because, as a group, they are older. Within each age group, subnational voters are better educated. Compared to national voters, the subnationals are more Protestant and Jewish and more White.

On the whole, the subnational electorate is more partisan and upper middle-class, while the national electorate is less strongly attached to a political party and lower in social status. These categoric differences between the two electorates are detailed in Table 2-7 and summarized in Table 2-8.

Table 2-7 Differing Compositions: National and Subnational Electorates

	Proportion of the Electorate	
	Subnational 1970	National 1972
Interest		
High	45%	39%
Medium	42%	44%
Low	13%	18%
Sense of Political Efficacy		
High	15%	14%
	21%	24%
	25%	22%
	21%	20%
Low	17%	19%
Strength of Partisanship		
Strong	35%	29%
Not Very Strong	39%	41%
Leaning	16%	22%
Independent	10%	9%
Party Preference		
Democratic	44%	41%
Independent	27%	31%
Republican	30%	28%
Subjective Social Class		
Working	47%	50%
Middle	53%	50%
Educational Level		
Grammar School	20%	15%
High School	47%	48%
College	28%	32%
Post-College	5%	5%
Occupation		
Unskilled	27%	29%
Skilled or Semi-Skilled	13%	14%
White-Collar	21%	21%
Professional and Managerial	39%	36%
Income		
$0 – $5,000	24%	20%
$5,000 – $10,000	30%	28%
$10,000 – $15,000	26%	26%
Over $15,000	20%	26%

Table 2-7 (cont.)

Sex		
Male	45%	45%
Female	55%	55%
Race		
White	92%	90%
Nonwhite	8%	10%
Religion		
Protestant	73%	71%
Catholic	24%	27%
Jewish	4%	2%
Age		
21-29	15%	22%
30-44	28%	27%
45-65	39%	35%
Over 65	18%	16%

The greater partisanship and social status of the subnational electorate make them unrepresentative of the population. Yet the greater frequency of state elections and the large number of public officials chosen make this electorate more normal. The subnational electorate troops to the polls with the greatest regularity and constitutes the base of any electoral turnout. Although they are core voters, they do not make up a small yet representative sample of the presidential year electorates. They differ along important political, socioeconomic, and demo-

Table 2-8   Subnational and National Electorates: Summary

Subnational Electorate	National Electorate
Higher Campaign Interest	Lower Campaign Interest
Higher Sense of Efficacy	Lower Sense of Efficacy
Stronger Partisan Identification	Weaker Partisan Identification
Fewer Independents	More Independents
More White Collar	More Blue Collar
More Protestant and Jewish	More Catholic
More White	More Nonwhite
Older	Younger

graphic dimensions.[8] In presidential elections, more people vote than is normal; and because of their weaker partisanship, these peripheral voters contribute to the greater volatility of presidential electoral results. While more representative of the whole population, they are politically more unstable: Often they are either shooed to the polls or attracted by the theatrics involved in the national election.

PRIMARY ELECTIONS

Party primaries—public elections within a political party to nominate a candidate for office—are lower in turnout and less representative of the population than either presidential or state elections. In the states where the primary is only the preliminary to a general election battle, turnout has averaged about 28%. In one-party Democratic states, where primary success is often tantamount to victory, turnout averages about 31% and is higher than in the general election.[9] In his study of states with competitive presidential primaries, Austin Ranney found that turnout averaged 39% (30% less than the general election turnout in 1948-1968). Moreover, these presidential primary electorates, like all primary electorates, are unrepresentative of the party's rank and file. Primary voters are older, higher in income and occupational status, and more active in a variety of civic, religious, and political organizations.[10]

These facts raise serious questions about the utility of primaries as a means of candidate selection. Candidates must satisfy highly atypical citizens who vote in primaries if they are to get the nomination. Such candidates, however, may not be

[8]Angus Campbell, "Surge and Decline: A Study of Electoral Change," *Public Opinion Quarterly,* 24 (Fall 1960), 397-418.

[9]These data are adapted from Austin Ranney, "Parties in State Politics," in *Politics in the American States: A Comparative Analysis,* 2nd ed., eds. Herbert Jacob and Kenneth N. Vines (Boston: Little, Brown, 1971), Table 3, p. 98.

[10]Austin Ranney, "Turnout and Representation in Presidential Primary Elections," *American Political Science Review* 66 (March 1972), 27.

popular with the typical party member, let alone with the electorate as a whole.

These findings concerning turnout support Lester Milbrath's observation that "persons who strongly identify with or intensely prefer a given party are more likely to participate actively in the political process."[11] In primaries, turnout is so low because the absence of the party label deprives the voter of an important symbolic motivation to join the fray. Those who do participate are socially and politically atypical people, with distinctive interests and political preferences. The same situation typifies low turnout state elections. Only in presidential elections do large numbers of the poor and uninterested yearn to vote.

IMPLICATIONS

The differences in turnout rates among social groups are politically crucial. They may determine who wins. Likewise, the success of a popular referendum may be decided as much by its timing as by its merits.

High turnout advantages some interests and disadvantages others. The lower the turnout, the more likely it is that the result will favor those who vote regularly. These are the middle-class professionals who believe in the good government ethic. They encourage public spirited campaigns to get-out-the-vote. Ironically, the people they prompt to vote are the least likely to support (or benefit from) good government policies.

The parties understand that maximum participation is not politically neutral. In contrast to indiscriminate appeals to vote, a well-run campaign organization concentrates on getting its likely supporters to the polls. The goal is to mobilize one's supporters, rarely to convert one's opponents. With the higher turnout rates of Republicans, it is not surprising that registration and voter drives are primarily a Democratic party activity.

[11]Lester W. Milbrath, *Political Participation* (Chicago: Rand McNally, 1965), p. 52.

The Democrats compensate with organization for what they lack in individual motivation.

Consider the fate of the New York State Equal Rights Amendment in 1975. Turnout strongly affected the result. Because local officials were being elected in the upstate counties but not in New York City, the amendment was defeated. Encouraged by party organizations that had an interest in the local election results, the upstaters voted at a significantly higher rate than those in New York City. Although polls showed that a majority of New York citizens favored the amendment, far more conservatives than liberals voted. The supporters of ERA failed to realize that rushing the amendment onto the 1975 ballot handicapped their cause. Had the amendment been voted on the following year, upstate and city turnout rates would have been more nearly equal, and the amendment might have passed. In this case as in all cases, elections are decided by the votes actually cast, not by those that might have been cast.

The consequences of nonvoting are particularly striking for the poor. Politicians campaign less intensively in poor areas and make fewer promises that can be redeemed after the election. Since politicians do not fear retaliation by poor nonvoters, social welfare programs are the first to be cut. The loss of governmental benefits is most serious during periods of budget reductions. With their greater need for government services, the poor should seek to influence public policy at every opportunity. The one political resource of the poor is numbers. Where all votes are counted equally, the numerical advantage can be decisive. Nonvoting simply throws the advantage away.

The low turnout in American elections has major implications for democratic theories about electoral reform. The assumption that broadened opportunities for popular decision making would result in greater mass participation has not been borne out empirically. It would seem that the greater availability of voting opportunities has had the opposite effect: It confronts the voters with too many demands. When rats have too many options in a maze, they sit down and defecate. Through nonvoting, the public acts in a similar fashion.

Nowhere is public confusion and frustration more apparent than in the primaries. Even where winning the primary is tantamount to winning the general election, voter turnout is abysmally low. The absence of the party label deprives the electorate of a crucial motivation to vote. Whatever the intent of electoral reforms, they have clearly been counterproductive; whatever the bad practices of the parties and their leaders in the past, they have a valuable role to play in the future.

CHAPTER THREE

Party Loyalty

Partisanship—often maligned, less often understood—is the key to understanding American politics. Besides stimulating healthy competition, parties give voting a meaning that transcends particular elections. The emotions and expectations associated with partisanship provide benchmarks for the voter to evaluate political promises and measure governmental performance. For the politicians, these attachments constitute a reservoir of ideas, symbols, and slogans for mobilizing electoral support and for railing against opponents. Partisan loyalty ties voter and politician into the political process.

For long periods, one party or the other has maintained a dominant political influence. This influence, however, has not been complete, nor has it prevented electoral deviations. The Republicans had majority status from the Civil War to the 1929 Depression; since 1930, the Democrats have had the majority. The voters shifted suddenly and dramatically between the Hoover-Smith election of 1928 and the Hoover-Roosevelt election of 1932. Whole social groups moved permanently into the Democratic column.

Black voting patterns demonstrate the effect of the 1932 party realignment. Where the vast majority of Blacks had voted for the party of Reconstruction for sixty years, they now vote for the party of the New Deal. One N.A.A.C.P. leader counseled its members to vote for Franklin Roosevelt with the advice: "Turn your pictures of Lincoln to the wall, the debt is paid in full." Black voters remain the most solidly Democratic group in their attachments and electoral support. Today, there might be pictures of John and Robert Kennedy flanking one of Martin Luther King.

Mass party switching is clearly exceptional. We notice these electoral realignments because they are such extraordinary political occurrences. The rule is partisan loyalty and durability. Fully two-thirds of the voters decide which party to support before the campaign begins![1] This suggests the influence of deeply rooted partisan attachments. An identification with one party or another colors many voters' perceptions of particular candidates and increases the likelihood of consistent party voting.

THE NATURE OF PARTY IDENTIFICATION

The partisan identifier does not approach each election with a completely open mind. A Republican is more likely to take political cues from other Republicans (especially from friends and relatives) and to evaluate these positively. The same is true of Democrats. These biases are particularly important because it has been found that most voters get the bulk of their political attitudes and information not from the media, where all candidates are likely to be reported equally, but rather from opinion leaders. Such individuals are more interested in politics, pay attention to the media, digest and interpret political information and pass it along to their friends and acquaintances.[2] At each step of this multi-stage information flow, the influence

[1] Paul F. Lazarsfeld, Bernard Berelson, and Hazel Gaudet, *The People's Choice* (New York: Duell, Sloan, and Pearce, 1944); and Bernard R. Berelson, Paul F. Lazarsfeld, and William N. McPhee, *Voting* (Chicago: University of Chicago Press, 1954).
[2] Berelson, Lazarsfeld, and McPhee, 109–15.

of party identification increases the likelihood that existing biases will be confirmed.

For the average voter, party identification simplifies and organizes the chaos of politics. Politics is a marginal concern for most people. Considering the variety of more pressing problems that demand attention and the generally indirect impact of government, this should not be surprising. Simultaneously, American politics is extremely complicated. Most of us do not have the time or the resources to make sense out of candidate posturing and rhetoric. Especially when voters are called upon to choose among candidates for many offices, partisanship enables them to generalize from previous experiences. It makes perfectly good sense for voters with established party preferences to vote their heritage unless they are persuaded otherwise. Party clarifies political complexities and makes voting manageable.[3]

Strong partisans are the most likely to be informed, to think and talk about politics, to have opinions on political issues, and to vote consistently from one election to the next. This means that the bulk of the swing in electoral results (the change in vote distributions that make for turnover in office) is coming from the least admirable voters. These "swingers" are far removed from the idealized Independent who weighs issues and candidates intelligently. Too often, they are ill-informed, little interested, and opinionless.

In the past twenty years, the division of the presidential vote has swung from a Democratic high of 61% in 1964 to a low of 38% in 1972. However, the distribution of party identification has been quite constant. As Table 3-1 shows, the Democrats have kept the emotional loyalty of about 45% of the electorate, while the Republican share has been a steady 25%. This gives

[3]The specter of electors trooping to the polls simply to register their inherited preferences is not very reassuring to advocates of responsive and responsible government. They may find some reassurance in the close connection between partisanship and socioeconomic status. Since people associate most frequently with those like themselves, political homogeneity within groups is the rule. Thus, even if voters are uncritically reacting to social pressure and parental inheritance, it may be a good thing. More often than not, such voters are supporting the party that is in their self-interest.

the Democrats an edge in any given election, although this advantage is partially offset by higher Republican turnout. More important is the rise in those identifying themselves as Independents. Their proportion of the electorate has risen from a low of 22% in 1952 to 35% in 1972. Independents now rank second to Democrats in voter identification. The significance of this development will be discussed at length later in the chapter.

Table 3-1 The Stability of Party Identification Distribution, 1952-1972

Party	Proportion of the Electorate					
	1952	1956	1960	1964	1968	1972
Democratic	47%	44%	46%	51%	45%	40%
Independent	22%	24%	23%	22%	29%	35%
Republican	27%	29%	27%	24%	24%	23%

GROUPS AND PARTY IDENTIFICATION

A country as ethnically, religiously, socially, and geographically diverse as the United States is bound to show corresponding political diversions. While no group is a voting monolith, many have the characteristics of a bloc. To speak of the labor and farm vote or of the Catholic and Black vote testifies to the political solidarity of these groups. Many distinctive groups have distinct partisan preferences, as do the residents of different regions.

The South, with its identifiable dialect, architecture, cuisine, and politics, is the most familiar. Post-Civil War reconstruction provided the glue for regional partisan solidarity. Since the Republican party was associated with freed slaves and carpetbaggers, native Southern Whites voted Democratic. In many states the Republican party virtually disappeared, and the only meaningful electoral competition took place in the Democratic party primaries. This loyalty persisted even as its causes receded into history. Only since the 1960s has the appeal to "vote as you fought" lost its strength. The Solid South has begun to break up and elect Republicans.

Three factors have contributed to the rise of Southern Republicanism. First, the liberal social policies of national Democratic administrations, especially concerning civil rights, resulted in Southern defections from Democratic presidential candidates. This led to Strom Thurmond's Dixiecrat candidacy in 1948; and to Southern support for Republican candidates in 1956, 1964, and 1972, and for George Wallace in 1968. Second, the belated economic development of the South has transformed its social and demographic character. Residents of the suburbs of Richmond, Atlanta, Nashville, and Birmingham share many of the same political concerns as their Northern counterparts and identify with Republican party policies. Third, many middle-class Northerners have moved to the South in the past twenty years, either for business or retirement reasons, and they have brought their Republicanism with them.

Table 3-2 shows the changes in the regional distributions of party identification between the 1950s and 1972. Although the South is dramatically less Democratic than it was twenty years ago, it is still the most solidly Democratic region in the country. The Republicans are strongest in the West and Midwest—regions that were the bulwarks of Union strength during the Civil War. These data also testify to a dramatic increase in the number of Independents in every region, but particularly in the South and Northeast.

Table 3-2 Relative Party Strength Differences: U.S. Regional

Party	Northeast 1950s	Northeast 1972	Midwest 1950s	Midwest 1972	South 1950s	South 1972	West 1950s	West 1972
Democratic	35%	35%	41%	36%	67%	50%	47%	39%
Independent	28%	41%	26%	37%	16%	30%	26%	34%
Republican	37%	24%	33%	27%	17%	20%	27%	27%

The distribution of party identification for different social groups is shown in Table 3-3. People who consider themselves working-class tend to identify themselves as Democrats, as do low income and blue collar workers. This points to the durability of the labor bedrock upon which Franklin Roosevelt built the New Deal. Middle-class, upper income, professional, and white-collar workers are the most likely to identify with the Republican party or as Independents. Republicans are also more likely to be White, Protestant, of Northern European extraction, and resident in small towns or suburbs.

While the regional differences stemming from the Civil War have gradually weakened (along with New Deal class distinc-

Table 3-3 Party Preference Variations According to Socioeconomic and Demographic Group Membership

	Party Preference		
	Democratic	Independent	Republican
Subjective Class			
Working	46%	34%	20%
Middle	35%	37%	30%
Income			
$0 – $5,000	47%	30%	23%
$5,000 – $10,000	43%	38%	19%
$10,000 – $15,000	41%	34%	25%
Over $15,000	32%	38%	31%
Occupation			
Unskilled	47%	36%	17%
Skilled and Semi-Skilled	41%	41%	18%
White-Collar	40%	37%	23%
Professional and Managerial	34%	33%	32%
Race			
White	37%	36%	27%
Nonwhite	69%	23%	8%
Religion			
Protestant	38%	34%	28%
Catholic	51%	35%	14%
Jewish	52%	38%	10%

tions), the partisan loyalties of some groups have solidified. Blacks are overwhelmingly Democratic—another effect of the Depression realignment, but one which has been reinforced by the positions of the parties on the civil rights questions of the 1950s and 1960s. The lower class position of many Blacks reinforces this tendency. Blackness, however, is a better predictor of Democratic party preference than is class alone. Similarly, the tendency of Roman Catholics to prefer the Democratic party is strengthened by their largely working-class backgrounds, although the tendency is strong regardless of current social class. The nineteenth century ties between Catholic immigrants and urban Democratic machines are still strong. Jews retain their solidly Democratic loyalty regardless of social class.

PARTY IDENTIFICATION AND VOTING

Party identification is at root a subjective phenomenon. It relates to a voter's sense of attachment or feeling of loyalty to a particular party. The more intense people's party identifications are, the greater is their concern about who wins and the greater is their interest in the electoral campaign (see Table 3-4). The real importance of party identification, however, is its impact on electoral choice. The stronger a person's party identification, the greater is the likelihood that he will vote. And, of course, it follows that it is also more likely that his vote will conform with his established loyalty.

Over 98% of the Democratic identifiers report that they usually vote Democratic for president, just as over 98% of the Republican identifiers report usually voting Republican. Nearly two-thirds of the strong identifiers (as opposed to one-third of the Independents) in Table 3-5 claim to have voted in every presidential election since they became eligible to vote. Only 4% of the strong identifiers, compared to 24% of the Independents, report never having voted for president. Strong partisan

Table 3-4 Evidence of Strong Partisanship Based Upon Interest and Concern

	Strength of Partisanship			
	Strong	Weak	Leaning	Independent
Interest in the Campaign				
High	39%	31%	22%	8%
Medium	20%	43%	24%	13%
Low	17%	44%	19%	20%
Concern About Outcome				
Cares a Great Deal Who Wins	33%	38%	19%	9%
Does not Care a Great Deal	13%	41%	25%	20%

identification provides an important incentive to participate in elections. Those identifying themselves as Independents are the least likely to vote consistently.

Independents (as well as weak partisans) are more likely to vote in the higher voltage presidential election than in the more subdued state variety. The larger number of uncommitted voters coming to the polls produces an electorate in which the distribution and impact of party identification is not normal. A comparison of the 1970 and 1972 electorates according to their distribution of party identification shows the off-year electorate to be generally more partisan, more Republican, and less

Table 3-5 Strong Partisanship and Regular Voting

	Strength of Partisanship			
	Strong	Weak	Leaning	Independent
Voted in All Previous Elections	61%	48%	50%	34%
Voted in Most Previous Elections	22%	26%	18%	18%
Voted in Some Previous Elections	13%	17%	15%	24%
Voted in No Previous Elections	4%	9%	16%	24%

Independent (Table 3-6). The political implications are clear. The higher turnout national electorate is more likely to reflect the Democratic party's majority status in voting for president and for the ticket as a whole. It is little wonder that the Democrats launch voter mobilization drives while the Republicans pray for rain—at least in the cities and the South.

Table 3-6 Composition of Off-Year and Presidential Year Electorates

Party Identification	Subnational 1970	National 1972
Strong Democrat	22%	16%
Weak Democrat	22%	25%
Leaning Democrat	9%	11%
Independent	10%	9%
Leaning Republican	8%	11%
Weak Republican	17%	15%
Strong Republican	13%	13%

As a stable psychological predisposition, party identification is a major determinant of the voter's partisan choice. Its influence is greatest in those electoral situations where possible confounding influences, such as emotional issues or dominating personalities, are absent. The parties are like great locomotives to which a number of candidacies are hitched—like so many boxcars. The variety, content, and merit of individual candidates varies, but their linkage to the train provides a unity and coherence that would be otherwise absent. Whether a partisan train is routed through, sidetracked, or derailed depends on the voters' judgment of its performance. Even when we say that a district is safe for a particular party, we mean only that this safety reflects popular approval of its performance, not an invulnerability to defeat.[4]

[4]David R. Mayhew, *Congress: The Electoral Connection* (New Haven: Yale University Press, 1974), 37.

Party voting is strongest in elections where the partisan label is the clearest signal and the strongest source of information to guide candidate choice. While a presidential candidate is the personification of his party and elicits strong partisan sentiments, the highly publicized campaign issues and personality factors diminish the influence attributable solely to party. The greater drama of the presidential campaign titilates a larger number of voters who would otherwise not participate. The result is an abnormal electorate in size, social composition, and partisan identity.

Table 3-7 reports the percentage of party identifiers voting consistently with their identifications for president, governor,

Table 3-7 Voting and Party Identification: Off-Year and Presidential Elections

Office	Proportion Voting Their Party Identification	
	Subnational 1970	National 1972
President		73%
Senator	88%	75%
Governor	83%	81%
Congressman	82%	81%

senator, and congressman in the 1970 and 1972 elections. Partisan voting is lowest in the choice of president. Since these campaigns make the greatest intrusion on the voter's consciousness, the influence of partisanship alone is less. Partisanship is generally strongest in non-presidential years—when the bulk of state voting occurs, but when the campaign receives less publicity. It is stronger for the more local candidates (governor and congressman) than for those more closely connected with the national campaign (senator and president). Party identification counts for more in the less dramatized non-presidential elections and in the less dramatic offices.

PARTISANSHIP AND INDEPENDENTS

With the electorate's increasing independence, the continued usefulness of partisanship as a predictor of voting activity is questionable. When 35% of the voters identify themselves as Independents, it is difficult to speak of a stable two-party division in political loyalty. Large numbers of voters are loyal to neither party, whatever their actual voting decisions may be. The most striking feature of this increasing independence is the partisan disaffection of the youngest voters.

Table 3-8 shows the distribution of partisan strength by age group. The youngest voters are twice as likely as the oldest to identify themselves as Independents. Conversely, they are less than half as likely to have a strong party attachment. The younger the voters, the more likely they are to have no partisan attachment. The older the voters, the more likely they are to have a strong party identification.

Table 3-8 Age and Party Identification

Age Group	Strong	Weak	Leaning	Independent
21-29	16%	33%	32%	18%
30-44	20%	40%	24%	16%
45-64	32%	43%	16%	9%
Over 65	40%	41%	12%	8%

Columns grouped under: Strength of Party Identification

One might expect that as a person persists in a party identification, it will tend to become ingrained. Older voters might develop a psychic attachment to a particular party from long, habitual support.[5] They would then be more likely to consider themselves strong identifiers rather than weak identifiers or Independents. If this is so, young voters may be expected to establish partisan attachments as they grow older. However, this is not the case. Rather, the levels of partisanship and

[5] Angus Campbell, Philip E. Converse, Warren E. Miller, and Donald E. Stokes, *The American Voter* (New York: John Wiley and Sons, 1960), 160-67.

independence established early remain relatively constant even as an age group grows older.

Figure 3-1 graphs the percentage of the youngest and oldest age groups reporting themselves as Independents during the period 1952 to 1972. Although the independence levels of both groups fluctuate, clear and distinct trends are present. The older voters (born in the period 1892-1901) showed the same low level of independence in 1952 as in 1972. More importantly, the youngest voters (born in the period 1922-1931) persisted in their high levels of independence during these twenty years. They did not grow more partisan as they aged. Once set early in life, the proportion of Independents in an age group changes little. Older voters have more intense partisanship not because of age but because they developed their party identifications during an intensely partisan period. The younger voters, on the other hand, came of age politically in a period of less clearly partisan rivalry.

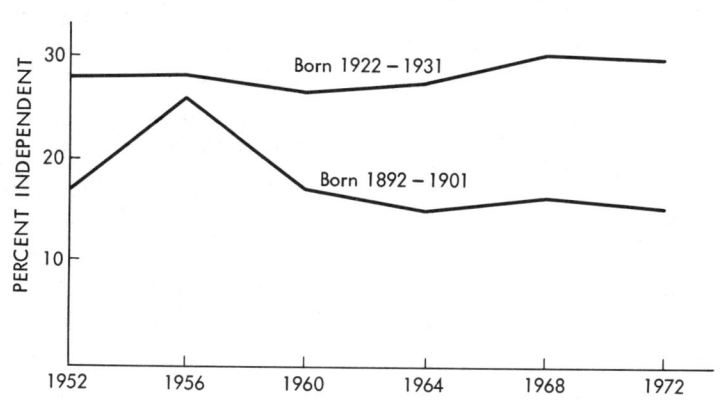

Figure 3-1   Proportion Independent: Age Group and Time Factors

This means that the effects of declining partisanship will be with us for a long time, as perhaps half or more of the voters identify themselves as Independents. The usual view of the

Independents has not been very flattering. They have been the least interested in politics, the least informed, and the least likely to discuss politics. They tended to shift back and forth between parties and in and out of the active electorate. This was not from conscious choice, but from an inability to establish clear loyalties or preferences. Independents were judged the least admirable voters.

The newly emerging Independents, however, are different. They reject the party system consciously as a response to political events, while remaining interested and continuing to vote. Their lack of trust in politicians and partisanship generally prompts voting for the candidate, not the party. Issues and ideology, along with personality, are the most important criteria for electoral judgment. Indeed, the new independence has emerged among the young, well educated, professional voters largely as a response to issues.

While many older Independent voters shared these characteristics, the present self-conscious Independent identification can be traced to post-1964 events—especially the Vietnam War and the Watergate scandal. Seeing one peace candidate after another escalate the war once he had been elected, and watching a president and vice-president forced to resign because of corruption and constitutional subversion, disillusioned many voters. The young were particularly affected because they were without the depth of loyalty developed over time. The large Independent identification is a "no" vote against a party system perceived as narrowly partisan, rather than as responsibly critical.

Earlier mass shifts in party loyalty (1860 and 1932) were to a new partisan allegiance. Whether the current no-partyism is a prelude to a major realignment is unclear. Given the persistence of early-formed levels of partisanship, it is likely that substantial anti-party sentiment will remain. There are good results: greater issue articulation by candidates, cleaner politics, a more highly discriminating electorate. On the other hand, these new Independents are devoid of the discipline, tolerance, and patience that party politics imposes. They are left defenseless against demogogic appeals which, regardless of ideological coloration, promise quick solutions to our problems.

IMPLICATIONS

Intense partisans report greater concern about who wins and a greater interest in electoral campaigns than do individuals with weaker identifications. Partisanship provides a psychological involvement in elections and makes politics exciting. For interpreting electoral swings, however, it presents a certain paradox. Those who are best informed and most interested are the ones who are least likely to change their votes. In a sense, the decision is left to the least qualified.

The distribution of partisan identification affects the parties' campaign strategies and electoral appeals. As the majority party in popular identification, the Democrats should encourage citizens to think about politics in partisan terms. By constantly linking candidate and party, Democrats may hope to capitalize on their advantage. Democrats should clearly advertise "Vote Democratic, Vote Smith" or "Vote Smith, Stevenson, and the Whole DEMOCRATIC TEAM." Since Democrats identify less strongly and vote less reliably, they also need the additional re-enforcement. For the Republicans, the practical imperative is to minimize the relevance of party in voters' decisions and to stress the candidates and issues. A Republican campaign poster might read "Vote Wilkie for Honest Government" or "Vote Wilkie, Landon, and Goldwater, A WINNING TEAM." Thus Richard Nixon's 1972 campaign organization was called the Committee to Re-Elect the President rather than Republicans for Nixon or even the National Republican Party. Nixon rarely drew attention to his partisan affiliation.

The use of party as an organizing principle is one of the causes of the coattail effect associated with presidential campaigns. All the candidates of a party are tarred with the brush of its presidential nominee. Such partisan generalizing casts individual elections as referenda on past party performance, not as judgments on the particular candidates involved. Coattail effects will decline as the importance of partisanship declines. Presidents have won electoral landslides yet have been unable to control either house of Congress. As people relate to politics less in terms of party, all coattails, whether Republican or Democratic, will shorten.

If the new Independents turn out to be antipartisan rather than merely nonpartisan, the trend will accelerate. If people react negatively to the whole idea of party, even Democrats will be forced to play down partisanship rather than alienate the uncommitted. For those hostile to partisan loyalty as an abdication of citizen duty, this may seem a significant improvement. Nevertheless, without the secure reference point of party, the votes of the less well informed will become more capricious and subject to greater manipulation by modern advertising techniques.

California presents one vision of the political style that might accompany a largely Independent electorate and a no-party political system. Devices such as cross-filing, whereby candidates could run in the primaries of both parties simultaneously, deprived California parties of organizational and ideological coherence. Voters are mobilized "through manipulative techniques—by sophisticated public-relations planning, by the deliberate management of images, phrases, symbols, by careful orchestration of emotions, by *ad hoc,* specialized, issue-oriented citizen or volunteer committees."[6] Traditional party loyalties mean very little. California's legacy is the technique of running campaigns without parties. The results have been mixed: Jerry Brown, Ronald Reagan, John Tunney, Richard Nixon.

[6]Theodore H. White, *Breach of Faith* (New York: Atheneum/Reader's Digest Press, 1975), pp. 52–53.

CHAPTER FOUR

Party Competition

Two-party competition is the bedrock of American democracy. Since the earliest days of our political history, dualistic rivalry has been the rule: Federalists versus anti-Federalists, Federalists versus Democratic-Republicans, Whigs versus Democrats, Republicans versus Democrats. The names have changed somewhat, group coalitions have shifted, and electoral success has varied; but the shape and competitiveness of the party system has endured.

Parties are essential to the operation of the American political process. They run candidates for office and structure the campaigns. Their labels serve as voting cues and their platforms define the issues. Parties also organize the government and direct the legislative process. A Democratic president will appoint Democrats to cabinet positions to pursue Democratic policies. A Republican Congress will have Republican leadership and further Republican interests. The parties make government responsible and link the voters to public policy-making.

By peopling the government and defining issues, the parties enable the voter to relate particular candidates to general principles. Amidst the clamor and transience of electoral campaigns, they allow new claims to be judged against past performance. As political institutions they offer a historical tradition, organizational durability, ideological flexibility, and a future orientation. Because they are more stable than a particular campaign, the parties tie politicians to the public and both politicians and the public to American political history.

THE AMERICAN PARTY SYSTEM

The Constitution does not call for two-party politics. In fact, parties are not mentioned at all. The Founding Fathers were profoundly suspicious of parties (or factions) as divisive forces. Nevertheless, an ultimate political realist like James Madison recognized that social and economic interests would vie for political power. Constitutional mechanisms such as separation of powers, checks and balances, and staggered elections were devised to safeguard the government against tyrannical factions. More fundamentally, ambition was to be allowed to check ambition; rival and opposite interests to compensate for the absence of higher motives.[1] The two-party system is a means for achieving such a political balance. One party serves as a watchdog over the other and thus acts as a sentinel for the public good.

Politicians do not usually see things in such philosophical terms. For them, competition is an unfortunate fact of political life. It is the awful price that one must pay in order to exercise statesmanship. For the rest of us, two-party competition permits a periodic replacement of one group of rascals with another. Nothing keeps an office holder more responsive than the specter of defeat. Nothing keeps a governing party more responsible than the existence of an alternative grouping ready to take over the conduct of public affairs. In sum, a competitive

---

[1]*The Federalist,* ed. Edward Mead Earle (New York: Random House, n.d.), Nos. 10 and 51.

two-party system promotes popular control over the government and enhances official accountability.

The two-party description of American politics, like all such generalizations, is somewhat oversimplified. There are Vegetarians, Prohibitionists, and Socialist Workers, not to mention New York's Liberals and Conservatives. More significant is George Wallace's American Independent Party that polled 13.5% of the vote in the 1968 Presidential election. Indeed, third parties like Free Soilers and Greenbacks have been powerful, if sporadic, forces in electorate politics. The Progressives early in the twentieth century and the Populists late in the nineteenth century had great regional success and saw their platforms adopted by the major parties. The Republicans are the most successful third party. A minor party when founded in 1854, by 1860 they had pushed the Whigs from office and captured the presidency in a four way election.

The ideological differences between the two parties, while never great, have not been constant. The debate between Alexander Hamilton and Thomas Jefferson in the Federalist era over loose versus strict construction loses its meaning as Hamilton's Republican successors advocate state's rights/limited government and contemporary Democrats speak for an interventionist central government. The parties have differed most consistently over monetary policy. Reflecting its Jacksonian ancestry, the Democratic party has historically favored the debtor with cheap money, state banks, low interest rates, free coinage of silver, inflation, and expansionary government spending. As befits its Hamiltonian heritage, the Republican party has stood for creditor interests: tight money, the National Bank, high interest rates, the gold standard, deflation, and restrictive government spending.

While the parties do not engage in ideological warfare, they are not Tweedledee and Tweedledum. Each has a quite distinct gravitational center and policy orientation. A Democratic administration is more likely to favor higher minimum wages, equal opportunity protections, income maintenance plans, and public housing. These programs are broadly termed the social welfare state. A Republican administration will generally propose investment tax credits, balanced budgets, lower taxes, and flexible regulatory policies. These are associated with the interests of modern capitalists.

These ideological differences reflect different bases of group appeal. The Democrats receive greater support from the poor, union members, recent immigrant groups, racial minorities, and the less well-educated urbanites. The Republicans receive their greatest support from the well-to-do, professionals and businessmen, older immigrant groups, Protestants, and the better educated residents of suburbs and small towns.[2] Democratic campaign appeals reflect its "have not" membership: cheap money, inflation, debtors' relief, social democracy. Republican appeals befit its "have" membership: tight money, deflation, creditor guarantees, enlightened capitalism. The Democrats are the party of change; the Republicans the party of order. The not so simple task confronting the public is to reduce these competing claims to a single vote for a specific candidate in a given election. Not surprisingly, voters tend to vote according to a general assessment of the goodness or badness of the times. The party in power when disaster strikes will be held accountable, whether correctly or not. Once victorious, a party will stay in for the duration of good times. Consequently, it is more accurate to say that the incumbent party loses an election rather than that the challenging party wins it.

COMPETITION IN THE STATES

The principal limitation on speaking of a two-party system is neither electoral nor ideological, but structural. Federalism,

[2] See Fred I. Greenstein, *The American Party System and the American People,* 2nd ed. (Englewood Cliffs: Prentice-Hall, 1970).

whereby the national and state governments are Constitutional coequals with powers distributed between them, is a powerful centrifugal force. To speak of two parties is a serious, if conventional, misnomer. The real number is more like 102: two national parties plus 100 state parties (two organizations in each state). More important, the locus of power is in the states, not in the national party organizations. The Democratic and Republican national committees are largely powerless paper organizations that mind the store between presidential nominating conventions.[3] Even these quadrennial events are essentially occasions when the state party organizations get together for nominating a winning presidential candidate and planning a national campaign.

Winning the White House can be to a state party's advantage if the candidate is popular in-state and if he is patronage-prone. Losing it, however, does not mean a party's doom, as is witnessed by Republican survival during the years from 1932 to 1952 and by the Democrats' consistent wins from 1860 to 1884. Since contests for all offices but the presidency are local, the key to electoral success is within the states. State parties recruit people into politics, provide the battlegrounds for nominating struggles, finance the general elections, and organize the government if they are victorious. The states are the focus of party organization, electoral competition, and voting activity.

To dominate American politics means to control a diverse coalition of state parties; to compete for this control means battling for state and local offices. Party competition is thus best considered in relation to the intensity of partisan struggle and to the frequency of success for state offices (governorships and legislative seats) rather than for federal posts. The potential for this competition varies from state to state and is strongly influenced by unique circumstances. As a general rule, however, competitive two-party states are substantially more urban and

---

[3]See Bernard C. Hennessy and Cornelius P. Cotter, *Politics Without Power* (New York: Atherton Press, 1964).

industrial than the noncompetitive states.[4] Figure 4-1 shows the fifty states categorized according to degree of competition: noncompetitive (one party wins virtually all the time), modified competitive (one party wins most of the time but the opposition has a chance), and competitive (a two-party horse race with evenly matched electoral successes).

The Civil War divisions are still evident in the Democratic party's domination of the Southern States. Regional solidarity, reactionary appeals, and racial fears have kept these states noncompetitive. On the other hand, the states that supported the Union are not one-party Republican strongholds. Moreover, the South's noncompetitiveness is declining as it becomes socioeconomically more like the rest of the country. The breakup of the Solid South is most evident in rapidly growing states like Florida and Virginia. The Republicans, however, have won governorships in Alabama and South Carolina and recently came within an eyelash of winning in Mississippi. Southern reconstruction is finally occurring, but in response to demographic and economic transformations rather than to army occupation.

Urban, industrialized states have a multiplicity of diverse groups for whose electoral support parties must compete, usually by promising better treatment. Rural, agrarian states are more socially, economically, and politically homogeneous. A single party can represent their more uniform values and widely shared political interests. Historical accident frequently explains which party is dominant. When cleavages exist in a state over which conflict can take place—rural/urban, city/suburban, agriculture/manufacturing, immigrant/native born, Black/White —parties will seek a winning electoral coalition by competing for the approval of a wide range of groups.

Pennsylvania typifies the competitive party system. No Northern state gave more of its citizens as soldiers for the Union cause or was as fought on. For long periods afterwards, efficient Republican party organizations kept the state safe for

[4]Austin Ranney, "Parties in State Politics" in *Politics in the American States: A Comparative Analysis,* 2nd ed., eds. Herbert Jacob and Kenneth Vines (Boston: Little, Brown, 1971), 90.

Figure 4-1 Party Competition in the American States

Noncompetitive (7)	Modified Competitive (15)	Competitive (28)
Louisiana	Florida	North Carolina	Hawaii	New Jersey
Alabama	Tennessee	Virginia	Rhode Island	Pennsylvania
Mississippi	Maryland	North Dakota	Massachusetts	Colorado
South Carolina	Oklahoma	Kansas	Alaska	Michigan
Texas	Missouri	New Hampshire	California	Utah
Georgia	Kentucky	South Dakota	Nebraska	Indiana
Arkansas	West Virginia	Vermont	Washington	Illinois
	New Mexico		Minnesota	Wisconsin
			Nevada	Idaho
			Connecticut	Iowa
			Delaware	Ohio
			Arizona	New York
			Montana	Maine
			Oregon	Wyoming

Source: Adapted from Austin Ranney, "Parties in State Politics," in Herbert Jacob and Kenneth N. Vines (eds.), Politics in the American States: A Comparative Analysis 3rd ed., p. 61. Copyright © 1976, 1971, 1965 by Little, Brown and Company (Inc.) Reprinted by permission.

the Grand Old Party by recalling the Grand Army of the Republic. In the post-Civil War period, Pennsylvania also became one of the country's most economically developed states. Philadelphia, always a city, became a great urban center (then the third largest); Pittsburgh, with the steel foundries and blast furnaces of the Monongahela River, is a synonym for industrialization. This social and economic development also produced a political transformation. The Keystone State is a classic case of intense and close two-party competition between Democratic Philadelphia and Pittsburgh at the geographic extremes and everything in between (except the coal region) that votes Republican. This typifies the competitive state: an equal number of safe districts from which the parties try to turn out as many voters as possible.

STATE POLITICAL BEHAVIOR

The competitive states generate more varied and more intense political stimuli than the noncompetitive states. The result is greater political interest among the voters, "not only because more stimuli are available for consumption, but also because interest rises with increasing conflict. People tend to follow a close contest with more interest."[5] Increased party competition is associated with higher voter turnout, greater public involvement in politics, and a more positive evaluation of the political process. When people are given a reason to be concerned about politics, they respond with heightened interest and activity. When the results of participation are perceived as meaningless or ritualistic, the voters opt out—formally and psychologically.

Table 4-1 shows the voting activity in competitive, modified competitive, and noncompetitive states in 1966 and 1970. The turnout levels reported in the competitive states are particularly

[5] Lester W. Milbrath, "Political Participation in the States," in *Politics in the American States,* 2nd ed., eds. Herbert Jacob and Kenneth Vines (Boston: Little, Brown, 1971), 50.

striking. While there are several factors besides party competition that may influence turnout, the differences shown in this table are still significant. Whatever the independent role of parties in the policy-making process, the effects of party competition on political behavior are far from minimal.[6]

Table 4-1 Voter Turnout: Types of States

	Proportion Voting	
	National 1966	Subnational 1970
Noncompetitive States	49%	48%
Modified Competitive States	56%	48%
Competitive States	66%	68%

While voting is far and above the most frequent form of public involvement in politics, political participation manifests itself in other ways. Table 4-2 shows the relationship between

Table 4-2 Political Participation: Types of States

	Proportion		
	Attending Political Meetings	Participating in a Political Campaign	Members of a Political Organization
Noncompetitive States	6%	4%	2%
Modified Competitive States	7%	5%	3%
Competitive States	11%	9%	7%

the degree of inter-party competition and three forms of political involvement: attendance at political meetings, participation in a political campaign, and membership in a political organization. In all three cases, less than 11% of the total electorate were involved. Nevertheless, there was greater involvement with

---

[6]See Sarah McCally Morehouse, "The State Political Party and the Policy-Making Process," *American Political Science Review* 67 (March 1973), 55–72, for a discussion of the role of parties and socioeconomic forces in state policymaking.

greater party competition. In each instance, increased voter activity accompanied increased party competitiveness.

The voters also have a range of evaluative attitudes concerning political performance. Such attitudes reflect their sense of subjective competence or political efficacy. Americans are generally efficacious compared to citizens of other nations. Table 4-3 indicates that these evaluations are also significantly related to the degree of inter-party competition. The higher the party competitiveness, the higher the feelings of personal political efficacy.

Table 4-3 Personal Political Efficacy and Voting Evaluation

	Proportion Agreeing			
	People Like Me Have No Political Power	Public Officials Do Not Care What People Like Me Think	Politics is too Complicated for People Like Me	Voting is an Effective Weapon
Noncompetitive States	45%	56%	81%	73%
Modified Competitive States	42%	53%	77%	68%
Competitive States	32%	44%	70%	55%

When asked their reaction to the statement "People like me have no political power," disagreement was voiced by greater numbers in the competitive than in the noncompetitive and modified competitive states. Feelings of political power increased with partisan competitiveness. Similarly, political cynicism was at its lowest in the most competitive states. The statement "Public officials do not care" elicited stronger disagreement in the competitive than in the noncompetitive or modified competitive states. The more competitive the state, the higher the trust in public officials.

Somewhat contradictory is the widespread agreement (between seventy and eighty per cent) that "Politics is too complicated for people like me." Although those in the competitive states were the least likely to agree, the agreement demonstrates generalized anxiety about the complexity of political issues.

Either political leaders fail to make the issues comprehensible or the issues are perceived as increasingly complex. Also surprising is the absence of an association between inter-party competition and positive evaluation of the electoral process. The relationship is inverse: As party competition increases, citizen agreement concerning the effectiveness of voting decreases.

This might result from the experience that people in one-party states have with consistently voting for winners—candidates of the dominant party. Voters in competitive states, on the other hand, have had mixed electoral success. Further, the state government may be typified by divided control of the executive and legislative branches, in addition to intra-branch divisions. This would blur any strong perception of voting as having an immediate political impact. The result is ambivalence toward voting as a means of political expression.

Stable two-party rivalry has clear political consequences. The electoral turnout is higher, citizen political involvement is greater, and feelings of personal political efficacy increase. As American politics becomes more competitive and less one-party dominated, these may become increasingly frequent characteristics. Public disbelief in the effectiveness of voting in the most competitive states and the growing absence of trust in government represent more disturbing developments. Perhaps reliance on party competition to insure public satisfaction is both simple-minded and narrowly conceived. Simplistic because it relies on a mechanism (inter-party competition) rather than a process (the representation of voter interests). Too narrow because it assumes that the voter will be content with formalities to the exclusion of tangible results. If government is perceived as ineffective, unrepresentative, and untrustworthy, party competition will not redeem it.

COMPETITIVENESS AND CANDIDATES

Increased reliance on party as a voting cue has not accompanied increased party competition. In fact, the opposite has occurred. Straight ticket voting has declined from about 60% in the 1950s to 45% in 1970. There has also been a 10% drop in the proportion of the voters supporting a congressional candidate consistent with their party identification. The voter is increasingly less self-conscious about voting inconsistencies and decreasingly loyal to a party.

Split control of government, where the executive and legislative branches are organized by different parties, is well established in American politics. In the period from 1946 to 1970, Congress and the presidency were controlled by different parties 40% of the time. In the same period, every non-Southern state experienced divided control (governorship and legislature controlled by different parties) at least once. For the competitive two-party states, divided control existed 50% of the time.[7] Thus the states most likely to satisfy the norm of stable competition are the least likely to have the unified control necessary for effective government.

Of course, there is no reason why a government (national or state) in which the legislative and executive branches are controlled by opposite parties cannot prosper. There are certainly occasions when the public good will triumph over partisan differences. These are, however, rare events—usually induced by a natural disaster or by external threat. Even the incidence of catastrophic depression and state bankruptcy has not deterred politics as usual or stimulated bipartisan cooperation. Bitter partisan conflicts and policy deadlocks have doomed more than one administration.

Governors are further hampered by the frequent incidence of independently elected executive department heads. This allows intra-branch partisan divisions to complicate those found between branches. Governors are thus forced to bargain for opposition party support in the execution, as well as the formulation, of public policy. Like the president, a governor may also have little real control over his own party officials. Control of party organizations is not only dispersed among the states but

---

[7] Ranney, "Parties in State Politics," p. 109.

also among the localities within the states.[8] Officials nominated and elected separately owe little or nothing to their nominal party chief and are free to pursue independent courses of action if they desire. A chief executive's power is greatest when his party has a slim legislative majority. In these situations, intraparty factionalism is minimized and executive leadership strengthened as the party rallies around its leaders in order to thwart the opposition. The best level of competition is just enough to preserve party solidarity without promoting internecine warfare either between or within parties.

For elections to serve as a mechanism for registering policy preferences as well as personnel selection, certain conditions must be met. Two programmatically distinct parties must compete for popular approval. One party must win control of both branches of government in order to implement its program. The realities of the American political system, however, work against the realization of such a responsible party government goal. These are structural (separate branches, long ballot) and behavioral (differential party voting). Nevertheless, if split control weakens clear party responsibility, it also testifies to the popular acceptability of both parties as alternative governments. Since either party might win the next election, both must behave as potential governments—responsible, moderate, centrist, pragmatic, flexible.

The strong ticket splitting in recent elections indicates that split control will be a fixture of American government. Besides its direct consequences for public policy-making, split ticket voting deeply influences the nature of political competition. When voters choose without regard to party, candidates will emphasize issues and/or personalities. If issues are stressed, this may lead to a more sophisticated and discerning electorate. On the other hand, split ticket voting may portend the disintegration of the party system in the face of public disaffection.

[8]Samuel J. Eldersveld, *Political Parties: A Behavioral Analysis* (Chicago: Rand McNally & Company, 1964).

Until comparatively recently, it was nearly impossible for the voters to choose candidates of more than one party. The political party organizations printed and distributed the ballots to be cast. Needless to say, each listed only its own slate. It was not until the introduction of the Australian ballot at the turn of the century that voters could choose the candidates of different parties in the secrecy of the voting booth. With the introduction of official ballots under government auspices, partisan neutrality replaced the "party polling place" atmosphere. The secrecy of voting also greatly reduced employer intimidation, machine pressures, and outright vote buying. Prospective buyers of votes could no longer be sure that the goods they bought were actually delivered.[9]

The curtained booth so familiar to present-day voters militated against blatant corruption. Its consequences went beyond the procedural by facilitating a transition from party voting to candidate voting. This change in voting behavior is illustrated in three ways. First, the percentage of the electorate casting split ticket ballots has grown from under 20% in the period from 1924 to 1944 to over 30% in the period from 1948 to 1968. The proportion of the public who voted for the same party for president in all elections for which they were eligible declined from almost 60% in 1956 to just over 45% in 1966. Third, in the same period the proportion of the electorate that voted a straight ticket for state and local offices fell from over 70% to 50%.[10]

Presidential voters cast split ballots more often than state voters; party identification predicts voting better in non-presidential elections. This should not be surprising. Smaller and more committed, the state electorate is more intensely partisan. It is also less influenced by the effects of presidential campaigning. The voters are more likely to defect from their normal

---

[9] See Jerrold G. Rusk, "The Effect of the Australian Ballot Reform on Split Ticket Voting, 1876-1908," *American Political Science Review* 64 (December 1970), 1220-38.

[10] Walter Dean Burnham, "The End of American Party Politics," *Trans-Action* (December 1969), 18-19.

partisan loyalties when prompted by widely publicized issues or deeply regarded personalities. The atypical presidential campaign generates publicity ordinarily absent in state and local elections. It also weakens party loyalty and undermines voting regularity.

A ticket splitting electorate necessitates certain changes in party campaign tactics. It will not suffice to whip the party faithful to the polls when they will not necessarily vote faithfully. Candidates must be attractively packaged. The advertising techniques for "the selling of the president" have been developed into a high art. This expensive merchandising of individual candidates exists to a lesser degree in gubernatorial and senatorial races, and is rare in races for lower level offices. But what about these elections? If party loyalty, regularity, and solidarity are weak or nonexistent, what serves as a voting cue? The answer can be summed up in a single word—incumbency.

Incumbents (those currently in office) are occasionally disadvantaged by identification with unpopular events, even those over which they have had no control. This was somewhat true for Republican congressmen with Watergate and for Democrats with the Vietnam War. Nevertheless, the advantages of incumbency strongly outweigh the disadvantages. First, incumbents are better known than their challengers, and people vote more frequently for the household name. Fewer than half the voters can name both candidates for Congress from their districts. Of those who can name only one, it is most often the incumbent.[11] Second, incumbents have had their entire terms to campaign for re-election; more especially, they have been able to address ostensibly nonpolitical gatherings as public servants, not politicians. The challenger, on the other hand, will not even have been nominated. Third, incumbents have greater access to the mass media, since they are newsworthy as public officials. Fourth, incumbents have time to build a secure basis of support

---

[11]Donald E. Stokes and Warren E. Miller, "Party Government and the Saliency of Congress," *Public Opinion Quarterly* 26 (Winter 1962), 531–47; Warren E. Miller and Donald E. Stokes, "Constituency Influence in Congress," *American Political Science Review* 57 (March 1963), 45–56.

within their party organizations and to establish a detailed election strategy. Fifth, most state legislatures engage in the bipartisan gerrymander whereby legislative district boundaries are drawn so as to guarantee the re-election of incumbents regardless of party. With these advantages, incumbents can survive partisan swings in election results, as well as shifts in their districts' partisan makeup. An incumbent's party thus reflects the distribution of party identification when he was first elected, as well as that when he was last re-elected.[12]

The cumulative effect of these incumbency advantages is striking. Incumbent members of Congress, regardless of party, are increasingly invulnerable to defeat, whatever the fate of the rest of the ticket. This insulates incumbents from adverse electoral results such as presidential landslides. As a result, the incidence of incumbents losing re-election contests has declined sharply, while the frequency of successful re-election campaigns has increased. While three-quarters of the congressional seats outside the South were competitive in 1932, only half were in 1964. By 1972, only one-third of the seats in the North and West were won with less than 60% of the vote. While election results were relatively uniform for different levels, a sharp distinction has developed between the partisan swing in presidential and congressional elections. The latter, when they involve incumbents of either party, are generally far outside the competitive range.[13]

This pattern of many strongly Democratic or strongly Republican districts and few districts in which the votes are evenly divided has several consequences. First, by insulating incumbents from shifts in the popular vote, it lessens the responsiveness of elected representatives. Second, it isolates the executive wing of the party from the legislative, thereby inhibiting inter-branch cooperation in public policy-making.

---

[12]See Andrew Cowart, "Electoral Choice in the American States," *American Political Science Review* 67 (September 1973), 835-53.

[13]Walter Dean Burnham, "Insulation and Responsiveness in Congressional Elections," *Political Science Quarterly* 90 (Fall 1975), 412-13, 424.

Third, it severs the connection that voting provides between public opinion and public policy as familiar names are returned again and again. Fourth, it erodes the responsibility of legislative parties and exacerbates the problem of split control. Fifth, by diminishing the influence of party loyalty, it leaves the voters without clear electoral guidelines.

COMPETITION WITHIN PARTIES

The weakening of party loyalties, the decline in inter-party competition at the local level, the growing noncorrespondence of national and subnational election outcomes—all affirm the primacy of candidates rather than party in electoral decisions. "Vote the person, not the party" has long been an honored, if unanalyzed, principle of American politics. In fact, people vote on the basis of a familiar name or image rather than on an informed judgment of a particular candidate's merits. The effects of partyless voting are clearly shown in primary elections.

The direct primary was a Progressive reform designed to eliminate machine rule and boss control over the nominating process. In these intra-party elections, competition takes place over who is to wear the party label in the general election. In the competitive two-party states, the primary is an expensive, time-consuming, and little understood preliminary event. In one-party states, or one-party areas of competitive states, the primary replaces the general election and usurps the opposition role from the minority party. The primary, however, is not the functional equivalent of the general election for one important reason. Candidates run as individuals, not as representatives of identifiable political institutions.

Two-thirds of the states require established party membership (registration) as a prerequisite for voting in primary elections. This strengthens the influence of organizational stalwarts (party regulars) and disenfranchises, or effectively denies the vote to, Independents (nonpartisans). It also prevents crossovers by opposition party members bent on choosing the weakest candidate against whom to campaign in the general election. Such an occurrence is possible in those states that allow primary participation without formal party affiliation: the so-called "open" primary as distinguished from the more common "closed" variety. Washington is unique among the states with its "blanket" primary—in which a registered voter may choose candidates from both parties, although he is allowed only one selection per office. Party influence has been effectively eliminated and some very peculiar candidates have emerged. Blanket primaries were devised to democratize the nominating procedure by maximizing popular access. Permitting opposition party and nonpartisan participation, however, has had quite another consequence. "Far from democratic, it is profoundly destructive of both the party system and the whole electoral scheme."[14] It overwhelmingly emphasizes name identification, which benefits incumbents and hinders the development of a responsible oppositon. Once in power, incumbents are usually insulated from shifts in public opinion. Of the four United States Senators with the most seniority, for example, two are from the one-party South (McClellan of Arkansas and Sparkman of Alabama), and two are from no-party Washington (Jackson and Magnusson).

Primary turnout is low both absolutely and in comparison to the national and subnational levels regardless of statewide competitiveness. This holds even for "one-party democracies" like New York City and Mississippi, where victory in the Democratic primary has traditionally been tantamount to general election victory. Primary campaigns are characterized by factionalism, personality feuds, and incoherence. Some one-party democracies have well-established intra-party groups with distinct ideological overtones (Longs versus anti-Longs in Louisiana and Reformers versus Regulars in New York City). The usual situation, however, is a dogfight of friends and

[14]*New York Times,* 26 August 1975, p. 30.

neighbors coalitions. The absence of the party labels renders the membership politically inert—deprived of the motivation and cues necessary for voting.

The primary also differs from the general election in the atypicality of its electorate. Just as the subnationals are not the presidential electorate writ small, the primary voters are no simple microcosm of the state party-at-large. Primary voters are older, whiter, more affluent, and better educated than either the national or subnational electorates. As V. O. Key Jr. warned, "the effective primary constituency may be a caricature of the entire party following,"[15] rather than the rank-and-file participation in party affairs envisioned by the Progressives.

Primary voters are, politically as well as demographically, unrepresentative. They are more likely to be true believers: people with intense, ideological, and nonpragmatic goals who are attracted to candidates appealing to narrow interests.[16] As the McGovern campaign suggests, highly contested primaries can greatly misrepresent the party membership.[17] While the turnout is higher in such primaries, it is not indicative of greater rank-and-file presence. Rather, large numbers of true believers inflate the lists; the result is an overrepresentation of the party's fringes.

Primary success too often depends on ideological purity rather than the candidate's attractiveness to the voters. Moreover, the requirements for victory in the general election are very different from those for the primary. Whatever their limitations, party leaders are interested in winning elections. They recognize that a candidate must be attractive to large numbers of Independents and persuadable opposition party members, as well as to the party's own membership. The suc-

---

[15]V. O. Key, Jr., *American State Politics: An Introduction* (New York: Alfred A. Knopf, 1956), p. 152.

[16]See James Q. Wilson, *The Amateur Democrats* (Chicago: University of Chicago Press, 1962).

[17]For another example see David W. Moore and C. Richard Hofstetter, "The Representativeness of Primary Elections: Ohio, 1968," *Polity* 21 (Winter 1973), 197-222.

cessful candidate in a competitive state is a person of broad centrist appeal capable of holding his own party together while attracting enough nonpartisan and opposition party support to gain the margin of victory.

A party whose nomination process is captured by ideologues often guarantees the opposition party's success (Goldwater in 1964, McGovern in 1972). However right candidates are on policy, they are wrong politically if they condemn their party to the electoral wilderness. Moreover, ideologically extreme candidates deprive the party membership of effective representation of their interests. They also narrowly circumscribe the political system by depriving the general electorate of meaningful alternatives from which to choose. A party that indulges itself in ideological excesses for a sustained period invites internal dissolution and/or the rise of a new party. In any case, the result is invariably candidates who are neither right nor president.

IMPLICATIONS

Competition between two rival claimants for political power is good. It is good because it keeps the governing class aware that they may face the specter of defeat. Politicians, quite simply, do not want to lose. They may consider Washington or the state capital a jungle, but they have no intention of leaving voluntarily. Competition is also good for the citizen. Voters in competitive two-party states are more likely to participate politically, to be informed about and interested in politics, and to have a strong sense of political efficacy. Competition generates concern about electoral outcomes that stimulates the public's involvement in politics.

Two-party competition, however, is largely a statewide phenomenon, even in the most competitive states. Classifying a state as competitive often means that there is an even split in the number of safe, one-party areas. Competitiveness in this sense is a partisan balance in the number of noncompetitive districts. New York and Illinois illustrate this phenomenon: an even division between the Democratic cities and the Republican farms and towns. The deciding element in statewide contests is the suburban areas where well-educated, middle-class residents are more likely to exhibit political independence. The mobility of these people, both social and geographic, has also loosened the ties of inherited party identification, making them less receptive to traditional partisan appeals.

The stability of party competition is also threatened by the decline in partisan loyalty as a decisive cue for voting decisions. Ticket splitting and electoral swings are evidence of increasing partisan ambiguities. At the same time, incumbents are increasingly impervious to electoral retribution. The results—split control and the insulation of incumbents—create a situation where parties are less responsible and government less responsive. Additionally, the large and growing proportion of the electorate that does not identify with either party bodes ill for the future of party politics.

The current disarray of American parties testifies to the unanticipated consequences of reform. This is not to fault the intentions of party reformers nor to condone political corruption. Procedural reforms, however, are not neutral. They invariably involve substantive readjustments in the distribution of, or access to, power. The Australian ballot guaranteed the ballot's secrecy, but it also diminished party voting. The primary broadened the candidate selection process, but it also allowed partisan extremists to veto candidates with strong general election appeal.

Consider the consequences of the long ballot. This procedure requires the election of a bewildering number of executive department heads: especially the chief fiscal and legal officers; often the chief educational officer, state auditor, and secretary of state. Most states also elect many judges; and all provide for the election of local officials, including mayors and county executives, city/town legislators, and local administrative officers as well as school boards, highway commissioners, and planning boards—to mention only a few. There are some 40,000 governmental units in the United States, almost all of which have elected officials. Jacksonian and Progressive reformers designed the long ballot to democratize government by making more officials responsible to the people. However, the complexity resulting from ballot length and the multiplicity of elections may have served to bewilder rather than to enlighten the electorate. There is certainly a marked fall-off in voter turnout from presidential to state to local to special elections; there is also a trailing off in voting from the major offices at the top of the ticket to lesser officials at the bottom. The inevitable ticket splitting leads to an everyone for himself political ethos that militates against intra-party cohesion and inter-party clarity.

Before we consign parties to the graveyard of political history, some observations are necessary. Despite the decline in partisanship, party still remains the strongest source of information about politics and the strongest determinant of electoral choice. Most people still identify with a party, and party identification remains a powerful influence on voting, especially at the subnational level.[18] Nor have political parties lost their critical representational role in American politics. As Walter Dean Burnham put it, ". . . political parties, with all their well-known human and structural shortcomings, are the only devices thus far invented by the wit of Western man that can, with some effectiveness, generate countervailing collective power on behalf of the many individual powerless against the relatively few who are individually or organizationally powerful."[19]

The complexity of American voting enhances the importance

---

[18] See Philip E. Converse, "Change in the American Electorate," in *The Human Meaning of Social Change,* eds. Angus Campbell and Philip E. Converse (New York: Russell Sage Foundation, 1972), pp. 263-337; and Jerrold G. Rusk, "The American Electoral Universe: Speculation and Evidence," *American Political Science Review* 68 (September 1974), 1028-49.

[19] Burnham, "The End of American Party Politics," 20.

of political parties for electoral choice. However complicated and numerous the choices and however ill-informed the voters, party provides a stable cue guiding the voter. While ballots are long and candidates transitory, the parties are durable, consistent reference points that can simplify complex electoral decisions. Parties are the primary instruments for electoral competition; wherever competition for political office exists (actually or potentially), political parties are organized to contest the elections. Indeed, what distinguishes democratic elections from their nondemocratic counterpart is the potential for competition. Parties serve to organize diffuse opposition into an alternative government. A complete team stands ready to replace those currently in office. This gives the voters some control (however indirect and circumscribed) over the content of public policy. The more the parties have to compete, the greater the opportunity for popular control, governmental responsibility, and public accountability.

CHAPTER
FIVE

Issues and Voters

Civics courses instruct us that issues are the stuff of political campaigns. Political practice, however, has consigned issues to the caboose of the campaign train. Party platforms, like campaign promises, have been the preserve of trivia experts and an opposition bent on embarrassment. Despite reams of newsprint discussing their importance and hours of television coverage discerning candidate positions, issues are usually considered to be of little electoral importance.[1] Rather, candidate obfuscation, party waffling, and voter fuzziness typify American political discourse.

What was Truman's position on 14B of the Taft-Hartley Law? (For repeal) Who raised the question of a missile gap in 1960? (Kennedy) What was Nixon's secret plan to end the Vietnam War? (It remained a secret.) The issues in political campaigns are like autumn leaves: They fall all around, gather into big clumps, and blow away until the cycle repeats itself. The voters' attention to issues is much the same as it is to the leaves: alert to what they signify but unaware of their individual meaning.

[1] Angus Campbell, Philip E. Converse, Warren E. Miller, and Donald E. Stokes, *The American Voter* (New York: John Wiley and Sons, 1960), pp. 168–265.

Nevertheless, issues are a traditional part of the electoral process. Newspaper editorials weigh their merits. Civic groups debate them. Candidates are expected to inform the voters of their views and translate those views into public policy if they are elected. Parties are supposed to provide well-developed alternatives between which the voter may choose. Issues make elections meaningful by infusing a policy dimension into candidate choice. In a representative democracy, issues make it possible for the electorate to evaluate the promises of candidates and parties and to judge their performance.[2]

American electoral politics has been periodically rent by great issue debates. Slavery in the 1850s, free coinage of silver in the 1890s, industrial reform in the 1910s, and social welfare in the 1930s confronted the voters with emotional and divisive questions. Race, Vietnam, and Watergate in the 1960s and early 1970s were issues of comparable intensity. Indeed, the duration and frequency of recent crises has been unprecedented in the post-World War II period. While crises are a recurring fact of political life, modern communications heighten public awareness of their existence and prompt politicians to offer panaceas. Does this mean that issues now have a greater impact on voting than previously assumed? Is the contemporary electorate better informed and more aware of issues? If so, what impact will this have on the electoral process?

ISSUE VOTING

If voters are asked "Is there anything about the parties or candidates that might make you want to vote for them?" 95% express clear likes and dislikes. When the total numbers of positive and negative judgments were compared, over 90% of the voters had an apparent preference for one candidate or party.[3] On the basis of this information, we might simply

---

[2]Austin Ranney, *The Doctrine of Responsible Party Government* (Urbana: University of Illinois Press, 1954)

[3]Stanley Kelley, Jr. and Thad W. Mirer, "The Simple Act of Voting," *American Political Science Review* 68 (June 1974), 572-91.

conclude that the most voting is issue based and that the winners' policy proposals had been endorsed by the public. Unfortunately, many of the issues reflected in these judgments hardly merit the name. Favoring a candidate because "He's a Democrat, and I've always been a Democrat," or because "I trust his smile," is not issue voting.

Issue voting involves meeting four conditions. First, the voters must have policy preferences. Second, they must distinguish party stands on the issues. Third, they must believe the policy stands of one party to be closer to their own. Fourth, they must vote for the candidate with whom they agree most closely. While stringent, these are minimum requirements. Even when voters do all four of them, we cannot say definitely that they voted on the basis of issues. There is a possibility that issue opinions are determined by partisanship rather than the other way around. Nevertheless, voters failing to meet all four requirements are not issue voters.

In order to determine the policy preferences and partisan perceptions of individual voters, we studied eight specific issues. These are: Vietnam, inflation, the rights of accused persons, urban unrest, campus disorders, industrial pollution, the rights of minorities, and government sponsored health insurance. (See the list of issue opinion questions, 1970 and 1972 on p. 87-90.) All have been the subject of heated public debate. Citizens' opinions about these issues will indicate their importance for voting.

PUBLIC OPINIONS

Most voters are opinionated. Two-thirds had opinions on all eight issues. Less than 10% failed to have opinions on at least six, as shown in Table 5-1. The difference in opinion levels between 1970 and 1972 is no greater than would be expected by chance. The excitement of the presidential campaign does not increase the number of voters with opinions on the issues. Paradoxically, the electorate that selects the most important shaper of public policy (the president) is not more interested in policy itself.

Table 5-1   Opinions and Issues

Number of Issues on Which an Opinion is Reported	Proportion of the Electorate	
	Subnational 1970	National 1972
8	70%	66%
7	15%	18%
6	6%	8%
5 or less	9%	8%

Most voters with policy preferences also think they know the positions of the parties and feel capable of identifying them. This is shown by the data in Table 5-2. In 1970, the voters were most aware of party stands on minority group aid. In 1972, the best known issue was Vietnam. The difference is completely predictable. In off-year elections, domestic issues most concern the voters.[4] Foreign policy issues are more likely to predominate in a presidential election.

The voters showed remarkable sophistication in placing the parties on an ideological dimension. This is shown in Table 5-3. People think that Democrats are generally more liberal than Republicans. This was especially true regarding Vietnam, aid to minorities, and government health insurance. Many voters were unable to distinguish party positions regarding pollution, the rights of the accused, and inflation. This suggests that such technical issues make little impression on the electorate. The voters were able, however, to make distinctions between the parties on the broad contours of public policy.

[4]Warren E. Miller and Donald E. Stokes, "Party Government and the Saliency of Congress," *Public Opinion Quarterly* 26 (Winter 1962), 531-47.

Table 5-2   Issues: People's Knowledge of Parties' Stances

| | Proportion of Those with Issue Opinions Assigning Parties a Position on the Issues ||||
| Issue | Subnational 1970 || National 1972 ||
	Democrat	Republican	Democrat	Republican
Urban Unrest	82%	82%	81%	82%
Vietnam	84%	86%	82%	84%
Campus Unrest	82%	85%	78%	80%
Minority Aid	89%	88%	79%	80%
Inflation	86%	87%	79%	79%
Rights of Accused	83%	84%	74%	77%
Pollution	84%	86%	70%	72%
Health Insurance	80%	80%	61%	62%

Vietnam was such an issue. Up until 1972, the voters shared the Democratic party's deep sense of confusion about the proper policy to support. Fully 25% of the electorate in 1970 thought the Democrats the more hawkish party. Two years

Table 5-3   Perception of Liberal or Conservative Stance

| | | Proportion Seeing |||
Issue		Democrats More Conservative	No Difference	Democrats More Liberal
Urban Unrest	1970	16%	33%	52%
	1972	12%	42%	46%
Vietnam	1970	26%	33%	40%
	1972	10%	20%	70%
Campus Unrest	1970	15%	39%	46%
	1972	9%	41%	49%
Minority Aid	1970	14%	35%	52%
	1972	11%	35%	54%
Inflation	1970	22%	33%	45%
	1972	31%	32%	37%
Rights of Accused	1970	12%	47%	42%
	1972	12%	47%	42%
Pollution	1970	14%	56%	32%
	1972	14%	57%	28%
Health Insurance	1970	10%	38%	53%
	1972	10%	32%	60%

later, there had been a dramatic crystallization of opinion. Only 10% of the voters saw the Democrats as hawks, while over 70% believed them more likely than the Republicans to favor immediate withdrawal. George McGovern's candidacy committed the Democratic party unequivocally to this position, and the voters took due note of it.

Such clarity is rare for American parties. Their wont is to blur specific issue differences while emphasizing nonspecific platitudes and/or the candidates' attractive personalities. As the parties actively campaign, they seek to grab the middle ground and so appear quite similar. Both will urge that we "Vote for Change" or "Elect a Young Dynamo." The complaint that the American people are given an echo rather than a choice has the ring of truth. Yet, when either party has deviated from the middle of the road (the Republicans in 1964, the Democrats in 1972), it has suffered a landslide defeat.

Large numbers of voters meet the first three requirements for issue voting: They have policy preferences, they think they know where the parties stand, and they prefer the position of one party. The proportion of the electorate simultaneously doing all three is shown for each issue in Table 5-4. Since a voter need meet these requirements for only one issue to be

Table 5-4   Issue Voting: Requirements

Issue	Proportion Who Have an Opinion and Prefer the Position of One Party on the Issues	
	Subnational 1970	National 1972
Urban Unrest	49%	39%
Vietnam	55%	59%
Campus Unrest	46%	40%
Minority Aid	52%	43%
Inflation	52%	45%
Rights of Accused	39%	32%
Pollution	33%	29%
Health Insurance	43%	40%

classified as a potential issue voter, over 87% of the electorates in both 1970 and 1972 might qualify. More important, people with issue preferences overwhelmingly vote for the appropriate party, as Table 5-5 documents for the Congressional vote. In sum, most voters in recent elections meet the minimal requirements for issue voting. Their opinions have been closer to one party's position than the other's. They have voted for the party whose policy stands were more to their liking. Elections have a claim as popular referenda on important issues. The winners may assert a popular mandate to put their promises into practice. They will usually do so anyway.

Table 5-5 Voting and Party Policies

	Proportion Preferring the Policies of a Party Voting for the Congressional Candidate of that Party			
Issue	Subnational 1970		National 1972	
	Dem.	Rep.	Dem.	Rep.
Urban Unrest	75%	63%	79%	57%
Vietnam	74%	68%	80%	58%
Campus Unrest	72%	68%	83%	62%
Minority Aid	76%	66%	77%	59%
Inflation	73%	69%	77%	58%
Rights of Accused	73%	61%	81%	56%
Pollution	73%	71%	79%	59%
Health Insurance	80%	68%	82%	62%

The relationship between issue preferences and candidate choice is stronger in the off-year elections than in the presidential election. The influx of less interested voters into the national electorate depresses the influence of issues. This has two consequences. Policy preferences are better predictors of vote in subnational races than in the national contests. Off-year elections better reflect the voters' policy views. The absence of the presidential campaign ballyhoo in subnational elections gives more interested voters time to reflect on the issues involved before casting their ballots.

The issue preferences considered here relate to national party images, not to the positions of local candidates. While local images and issues are sometimes important, this is unusual. For candidate stands to influence electoral choice, they must be recognized by the voters. Most voters, however, do not know where local candidates stand. Below the statewide level, many citizens fail to recognize the name of the incumbent, let alone that of his challenger.

Familiar names are a definite advantage. Sons and widows of popular politicians are regularly beneficiaries. Sometimes candidate and namesake may be less directly connected. In 1962, an otherwise unemployed factory worker with the same name as John F. Kennedy entered the Massachusetts Democratic primary for state treasurer. He won the primary and went on to beat the incumbent in the general election. When the voters were asked why they voted for him, many replied that they approved of his job in Washington. While bewildered about his decision to leave the White House for such a minor office, they were prepared to concur with President Kennedy's wishes regardless!

Local issues do occasionally play a major electoral role, especially if a candidate has been found in the wrong bed or at the end of a payoff. The national media, which dominate political reporting, ignore local candidates and their policy views. City-wide newspapers and television stations will cover the mayor's election but not the election of seven Congressmen or the forty state legislators. Rural politicians may not be local enough to be covered by the small town papers in their districts. Accordingly, voters respond to local candidates as partisan figures. This is ordinarily the only information available.

When Hymie Schorenstein was a sachem of New York City's Tammany Hall, he was once confronted by a new nominee concerned about election. Nowhere did advertising appear touting his qualifications (doubtless high) to be city coroner. As the young man's anxiety heightened, Schorenstein gave him a visual demonstration of local office electioneering. Pointing to the debris that was pulled in with an arriving ferry boat, the party leader observed: "Franklin Roosevelt is your ferry boat, and you come in with him." The lesson was not pretty—but it was accurate.

ISSUES AND PARTY IDENTIFICATION

For most people, issue preferences and party identification are complementary or at least not antagonistic. Only a small minority identify with one party while preferring the policy stands of another. Such cross-pressured people are mostly Southern Democrats. Partisan identification generally coincides with a consistent stand on specific issues. The average Democrat is consistently more liberal than the average Republican. Accordingly, Democrats are more likely to favor immediate withdrawal from Vietnam, federal action to solve the problems of unemployment and poverty, aiding minority groups, stopping inflation, and guaranteeing health care. Independents almost always rank in the middle; Republicans opt, on the average, for the most conservative policies.

While the average Democrat is more liberal than the average Republican, the parties overlap ideologically. There are Democrats who are more conservative than the average Republican—like, for example, John Stennis of Alabama. Conversely, there are Republicans, like Jacob Javits of New York, who are more liberal than the average Democrat. Consequently, both parties converge at a more moderate, centrist position. While extremists of both partisan and ideological persuasions exist, the parties as wholes are solidly in the middle of the road.

That Democratic identifiers prefer the more liberal policies of Democratic candidates says nothing about cause. The Democratic party may be reflecting the views of its supporters in adopting a more liberal position, or people may be supporting the Democratic party because of the policy stands it has taken.

In either case, election results would accurately reflect the voters' policy preferences. Alternatively, people may be both Democrats and liberals (or Republicans and conservatives) from parental inheritance. While this makes the connection between electoral outcomes and public policy more tenuous, these inherited preferences must be satisfied nonetheless.

Party identification may also distort political perceptions. Democratic identifiers may be fervent but uncritical supporters of liberal policy views because they are the views espoused by *their* leaders. Party identifiers see greater differences between themselves and opposition party members. Such partisans stereotype the opposition as extremist, while seeing their own party as more moderate.[5] By exaggerating the extremism of the other party, they are more likely to support the issue stands of their own. Unfortunately, this can be a self-fulfilling prophecy. Democratic identifiers may take the issue stands proclaimed by the party without accurately assessing the alternatives.

Party identification gives politicians a certain maneuverability in taking stands on the issues. Nevertheless, they must either please their constituents or face electoral defeat. No district is so safe for a party that officeholders can ignore public opinion or take issue stands consistently at odds with those who elected them. While voters' deciding on the basis of partisanship allows politicians some freedom, dramatic groundswells of opposition may arise if politicians ignore the wishes of their constituents too often or on too important an issue. The political graveyard is lined with politicians who put statesmanship above mundane local pressures. As Harry Truman once observed, statesman is simply another name for a defeated politician.

---

[5]This conclusion is based on a comparison of the mean positions assigned to the parties by each group of partisans, with the means based on the total sample. Democrats consistently assigned a higher (more conservative) score to the Republican party than did Republican identifiers—and conversely.

THE RATIONAL VOTER

Studies of mass electoral behavior conducted in the 1950s revealed shockingly low levels of issue awareness. Most voters were opinionless or had opinions that were extremely unstable. Only about a third could be called issue voters. A common conclusion was that average citizens were intellectually incapable of dealing with complex issues.[6] This explanation, however, is deceptive. Voters can only react to the issues of their times. If no serious problems threaten, why should voters pay attention to issues? If party differences are nonexistent, why bother to be informed?

Looking back, the 1950s seem made to inspire political apathy. Even during the Eisenhower recessions and the periods of brinksmanship, the future appeared promising to most Americans. On many policy questions, White House leadership was either lacking or incoherent. In contrast to the New Deal and the Fair Deal before it and the New Frontier and the Great Society after it, the Eisenhower administration had no positive theme. Intellectuals proclaimed ideology dead; politicians and public alike were complacent; politics became remarkably dull.

Civil rights, Vietnam, and the war on poverty changed all this. Issues and ideologies were hotly debated. Especially in the presidential elections of 1964 and 1972 and in the 1968 Democratic primaries, candidates took obviously different issue positions. Given a dialogue between competing viewpoints, voters became more interested in policy, and their opinions acquired a new consistency.[7] With a clear division of opinion between the two parties, voters were perfectly capable of understanding policy questions and reacting intelligently. The relationship between issue preference and voting choice has become

---

[6] Philip E. Converse, "The Nature of Belief Systems in Mass Publics," in *Ideology and Discontent,* ed. David E. Apter (New York: Free Press, 1964), 206–61.

[7] Stephen Earl Bennet, "Consistency Among the Public's Social Welfare Policy Attitudes in the 1960s," *American Journal of Political Science* 17 (August 1973), 544–70.

stronger as that between party identification and vote has become weaker.

How much attention should voters pay to issues? American folklore glorifies the rational voter who comprehends policy sufficiently well to compare the candidates across several issues. Such a voter assesses the candidates and their policies, gathers the necessary information, evaluates the campaign promises, and weighs the probable consequences of alternative policies. All of this is done objectively and with an open mind. When not in total agreement with either party, the rational voter can decide whether agreement with the Democrats on social welfare policy is more or less important than agreement with the Republicans on foreign policy. Final candidate choice involves a decision about which party will deliver the more desirable policy outcomes.

Not surprisingly, there are few such idealized voters, even among political science professors. Campaigns frequently obscure rather than clarify issues. Indeed, ambiguity can be a candidate's best strategy. Since American parties lack ideological cohesion and legislative discipline, it is usually difficult to assess the likely result of a candidate's victory. Even perfect information would not guarantee perfect prediction. Moreover, few voters have either the resources or the inclination to engage in such a search. The price is prohibitive and the gain problematic.

If the costs of good information are high and the rewards offered are low, rationality dictates using various short cuts for political decision making. Trusting the opinions of family or friends may be more reasonable than ferreting out the information necessary to form one's own opinions. Selecting a candidate on the basis of general ability or character makes more sense than attempting to guess future issue stands. Generalizing from the goodness or badness of the times is a satisfactory basis for voting when detailed analysis is impossible. Relying on party images (Democrats = prosperity and war; Republicans = peace and recession) may yield more accurate policy predictions than attempts to evaluate specific platforms. The voters may be ill-informed, but they are not necessarily stupid.

IMPLICATIONS

That political problems are complex and of marginal concern to most voters most of the time is an inescapable fact. This puts a particular responsibility on the media and on politicians to explain issues in ways that the average voter can readily grasp. When issues are clearly presented, and significantly different alternatives offered, the voters react responsibly. If issues are obscured and differences blurred, the voters react erratically and quickly lose interest.

The 1948 election presents an especially clear case. The press and the president saw this election as a referendum on Section 14B of the Taft-Hartley Act which outlawed closed-shop union agreements. Polls discovered that most voters had never heard of 14B. Worse, because 14B was labelled the "right to work law," many had the positions of the parties reversed. Some people, basing their votes on opposition to Taft-Hartley, voted for Dewey. Luckily for Truman, he also fulminated against a "Do Nothing" Republican Congress. While the accusation was unfair, many people liked Truman's feistiness and voted for him. Despite the impression given by the media, 14B had little to do with voters' decisions.

Average citizens think about politics in broad terms. They are neither adequately trained nor sufficiently informed to decide narrow questions. That is what they pay politicians to do. When confronted with the technical language of a popular referendum, many are incapable of understanding its precise meaning, let alone of understanding the implications of adoption or rejection. The catch phrase by which the question becomes known may prove more important than its substance. This can be dangerously misleading. "Right to Work" stands for weak unions; "Right to Life" means prohibition of abortions. People may favor the sentiment expressed by the phrase, yet be opposed to the actual ballot proposal.

Because of the low visibility of local issues, party is central to subnational electoral decisions. This means that state legislative and Congressional elections are frequently determined by the public's response to the chief executive and the general state of the economy.[8] With the exception of television personalities (like House Judiciary Committee members), a legislator's stands on individual issues are largely unknown. Even Congressmen who vote against their party will have its issue positions attributed to them by their constituents.

The vote is a potent but crude weapon. The elector can only vote yes or no, Democratic or Republican. Someone who is forced to make so basic a choice must think in basics. It is the politician's job to frame simple, yet comprehensive, alternatives between which citizens may choose. The voters, in turn, allow politicians to make policy without undue interference. They only demand that politics be kept within certain bounds. Vietnam and Watergate demonstrated that if these bounds are exceeded citizens are prepared to intervene actively. Americans may be politically docile and ill-informed, but they realize that politics is sometimes too important to be left to politicians. There is firm evidence for "the perverse and unorthodox argument . . . that the voters are not fools."[9]

APPENDIX

ISSUE OPINION QUESTIONS, 1970 AND 1972

Urban Unrest

There is much discussion about the best way to deal with the problem of urban unrest and rioting. Some say it is more important to use all available force to maintain law and order—no matter what results. Others say it is more important to

---

[8]Edward R. Tufte, "Determinants of the Outcomes of Midterm Congressional Elections," *American Political Science Review* 69 (September 1975), 812–26.

[9]V. O. Key, Jr., *The Responsible Electorate: Rationality in Presidential Voting 1936–1960* (New York: Vintage Books, 1968), 7.

correct the problems of poverty and unemployment that give rise to the disturbances. And, of course, other people have opinions in between. Suppose the people who stress doing more about the problems of poverty and unemployment are at one end of this scale—at point number 1. And suppose the people who stress the use of force are at the other end—at point number 7. Where would you place yourself on this scale?

SOLVE PROBLEMS OF POVERTY AND UNEMPLOYMENT } 1 2 3 4 5 6 7 { USE ALL AVAILABLE FORCE

Vietnam

There is much talk about "hawks" and "doves" in connection with Vietnam, and considerable disagreement as to what action the United States should take in Vietnam. Some people think we should do everything necessary to win a complete military victory, no matter what results. Some people think we should withdraw completely from Vietnam right now, no matter what results. And, of course, other people have opinions somewhere between these two extremes. Suppose the people who support an immediate withdrawal are at one end of this scale at point number 1. And suppose the people who support a complete military victory are at the other end of the scale at point number 7. Where would you place yourself on this scale?

IMMEDIATE WITHDRAWAL } 1 2 3 4 5 6 7 { COMPLETE MILITARY VICTORY

Campus Unrest

Some people are pretty upset about rioting and disturbances on college campuses and in high schools. Some feel sympathetic with the students and faculty who take part in these disturbances. Others think the schools should use the police and the National Guard to prevent or stop disturbances. And others fall somewhere between these extremes. Where would you place yourself on this scale, or haven't you thought much about this?

SYMPATHETIC WITH STUDENTS AND FACULTY } 1 2 3 4 5 6 7 { USE FORCE TO STOP DISTURBANCES

Minority Aid

Some people feel that the government in Washington should make every possible effort to improve the social and economic position of Negroes and other minority groups. Other people feel that the government should not make any special effort to help minority peoples but that they should be expected to help themselves. Where would you place yourself on this scale, or haven't you thought much about this?

GOVERNMENT HELP MINORITY GROUPS } 1 2 3 4 5 6 7 { MINORITY GROUPS HELP THEMSELVES

Inflation

There is a great deal of talk these days about rising prices and the cost of living in general. Some feel that the problem of inflation is temporary and that no government action is necessary. Others say that the government must do everything possible to combat the problem of inflation immediately or it will get worse. Where would you place yourself on this scale, or haven't you thought much about this?

TOTAL GOVERNMENT ACTION AGAINST INFLATION } 1 2 3 4 5 6 7 { NO GOVERNMENT ACTION AGAINST INFLATION

Rights of Accused

Some people are primarily concerned with doing everything possible to protect the legal rights of those accused of committing crimes. Others feel that it is more important to stop criminal activity even at the risk of reducing the rights of the accused. Where would you place yourself on this scale, or haven't you thought much about this?

PROTECT RIGHTS OF THE ACCUSED } 1 2 3 4 5 6 7 { STOP CRIME REGARDLESS OF RIGHTS OF ACCUSED

Pollution

There are many sources of air and water pollution; one of them is private industry. Some say the government should force private industry to stop its polluting. Others believe industries should be left alone to handle these matters in their own way. Given these two approaches, where would you place yourself on this scale, or haven't you thought much about this?

GOVERNMENT FORCE PRIVATE INDUSTRY TO STOP POLLUTING } 1 2 3 4 5 6 7 { INDUSTRIES SHOULD HANDLE POLLUTION IN THEIR OWN WAY

Health Insurance

There is much concern about the rapid rise in medical and hospital costs. Some feel there should be a government health insurance plan which would cover all medical and hospital expenses. Others feel that medical expenses should be paid by individuals and through private insurance like Blue Cross. Where would you place yourself on this scale, or haven't you thought much about this?

GOVERNMENT INSURANCE PLAN } 1 2 3 4 5 6 7 { PRIVATE INSURANCE PLANS

CHAPTER SIX

Values and Voters

Party identification fixes the voter's general political orientation. Issues can influence the voting decision in a particular election. Nevertheless, many election results reflect the collective experiences of the American public. People do not develop either party identification or issue opinions in an environmental vacuum. These concepts may be abstractions but they are learned concretely and stand for real concerns.

We are all born into a certain social milieu from which we derive most of our fundamental political attitudes. Those around us convey (usually unconsciously) judgments about what is politically good or bad and the real implications of political rhetoric. Whether we are inclined to view politics as instrumental, government as benign, and policy as the public interest depends largely on our life experiences and environmental conditioning.

POLITICAL SOCIALIZATION

Every society has a pattern of attitudes regarding political activity, governmental authority, and ideological beliefs that can be termed its political culture. Like all cultural orientations (courtship, childrearing, work and leisure habits, religious practices), it is passed on from generation to generation in a variety of nonapparent fashions. The process by which an individual receives these societally approved attitudes towards politics is called political socialization.[1]

We are socialized into the political community by learning and internalizing its values. Very few political beliefs are intuitively obvious, logically necessary, or historically inevitable. Some prior knowledge is necessary in order to interpret political events and make sense of them as guides to action. Things come together through the application of conventional wisdom, or, more accurately, through the application of conventionally learned wisdom.[2]

Political values like partisanship, and citizen duties like voting, are only rarely consciously decided or substantively altered. Of course, specific experiences may lead to a modification of these attitudes. Nevertheless, to a degree that discomforts our somewhat naive rationalism, we are the creatures of culturally defined values.[3] We are not mindlessly determined cogs, but culturally conditioned citizens. Our reactions to political events are filtered through socialized attitudes and tested against culturally defined values.

We are also very defensive when our values are threatened. Especially during critical periods, we cling to them often in the face of overwhelming contrary evidence. As then Representative Landgrebe exclaimed during the Nixon impeachment proceedings, "Don't confuse me with facts. My mind is made up." Clearly, the congressman did not choose to have his value system

[1] See David Easton and Jack Dennis, *Children in the Political System: Origins of Political Legitimacy* (New York: McGraw Hill Book Company, 1969); and Fred I. Greenstein, *Children in Politics* (New Haven: Yale University Press, 1965).

[2] Philip E. Converse, "The Nature of Belief Systems in Mass Publics," in *Ideology and Discontent,* ed. David Apter (New York: The Free Press of Glencoe, 1964), 212.

[3] Sidney Verba, "Conclusion: Comparative Political Culture," in *Political Culture and Political Development,* eds. Lucien W. Pye and Sidney Verba (Princeton: Princeton University Press, 1965), 513.

threatened. On the other hand, his constituents in Indiana saw fit to dispense with his services in the next election.

Like most other norms governing values and behavior, political socialization is conservative. It tends to conform to customary usage and to the instinct of people to want the future to reflect their own beliefs. It takes a cataclysmic event to disrupt the stable transmission of values from one generation to the next. The most difficult task facing a change-oriented government (revolutionary or reformist) is to re-educate people politically, to create a new political culture. In the face of popular opposition, such governments invariably give up on adults and concentrate their efforts on the young. Invariably, the revolutionary generation will seek to perpetuate its values by bringing up their children to be like themselves.

The political cultures of totalitarian countries are the most comprehensive and the least susceptible to change. In these societies, the state consciously coordinates all aspects of a person's life, as well as policies pertaining to economics, politics, and public welfare. In particular, these policies are determined with reference to an ideology or belief system. Noncompliance with the official culture is not just dissent, but a threat to the state. While totalitarian states are never completely successful in controlling the lives of their citizens, their coercive efforts are very different from socialization in nondictatorial countries.

Political socialization in the United States (and other democratic countries) is haphazard by comparison. The state is one of the many socializers sharing influence with family, peer groups, and secondary associations like unions and churches. Even in the public schools, there is little systematic indoctrination (beyond the daily pledge of allegiance); nor is there a rigorous ideology. The pressure for conformity to dominant political values is more informal. In particular, we are under strong pressures not to deviate from the opinions of those with whom we associate. Political socialization is thus a continuing process. It would only stop if a person were completely isolated.

Children pick up political values early in life from their parents. Party identification, in particular, develops from hearing one party or the other favorably discussed. The crux of parental influence is agreement. Children overwhelmingly have the same partisan identity as their parents. Fewer than 20% of American children who can identify the partisanship of their parents deviate from it. Children whose parents have different party identifications are the most likely to be Independents. If they opt for a party preference, it is more likely to be the mother's.[4] On the other hand, such strong-willed women have been rare. Most wives bring their political views into conformity with their husbands' politics.

Children learn that they are Democrats or Republicans before they have understood specifically why. These partisan loyalties also predate any understanding of the government as an institution. The first awareness that children have of government is highly personal. They see the president as a benevolent father-figure. Watergate, however, has caused a major disillusionment among young children concerning presidential benevolence and authority generally.[5] Whether the initial image is favorable or negative, only later do children begin to see the government as an institution and officials as a category of people called politicians.

The schools inculcate respect for established authority and build a favorable image of the state through citizenship education programs. Saluting the flag and singing the national anthem inculcate a sense of national oneness. Having historical figures to look up to and recounting their feats (like the story of George Washington and the cherry tree) create a national folklore and a sense of historical continuity. Electing class officers and organizing a student government establish precedents for

---

[4]Kenneth P. Langton and M. Kent Jennings, "Mothers Versus Fathers in the Formation of Political Orientations," in Kenneth P. Langton, *Political Socialization* (New York: Oxford University Press, 1969), 52-83.

[5]F. Christopher Arterton, "The Impact of Watergate on Children's Attitudes Toward Political Authority," *Political Science Quarterly* 89 (June 1974), 269-85.

majority rule and popular participation. Studying American history and the Constitution familiarizes students with current events and the problems of democracy.

Not all the socializing forces in American society reinforce passive acceptance of governmental authority. The intricate network of interest groups that typify American politics provides legitimate vehicles to make demands and to express dissent. Unions, for example, tie their members into a value system ("union brotherhood") while organizing to press for economic betterment. This takes place within the broader framework of American political culture and without challenging the government's legitimacy, even if its policies are bitterly denounced.

Political movements that threaten deeply held values elicit extremely emotional responses. Life style issues like drug use and sexual behavior involve clashes over fundamental questions of right and wrong. People who hold extreme counter-cultural views seem to threaten the value system of others, especially if those views are flaunted in a deliberately (and perhaps needlessly) provocative manner. While the flag is only a symbol without intrinsic value, to many it is a deeply regarded symbol of national unity and historical identity. Desecration of the flag is thus bad politics, even if it is or involves Constitutionally protected symbolic speech.

AMERICAN POLITICAL CULTURE

American self-consciousness about its political identity should not be surprising. The United States is a relatively new nation and one composed of people with diverse backgrounds. Despite the hegemony of White-Anglo-Saxon-Protestant values, these are by no means monopolistic. The melting pot description of American self-consciousness about its political identity should inaccuracy. Bouillabaisse would be a better culinary analogy: a rich stew in which the constituent elements retain their distinctive flavors.

There are elements of a national culture shaped by common historical heritage. The American Revolution and the Frontier have exerted a strong and persistent influence on all Americans, regardless of ethnic, religious, or regional background. The 1929 Depression and World War II offer more recent examples of such influence. Of course, there has been the experience of a common government and body of laws. Moreover, Americans share a high sense of political efficacy, a political openness and social trust, and a tolerance for dissent that defines their national political culture.[6]

Nonetheless, within this basic American political culture, there exists a wide variety of subtypes. These have distinct regional overtones, since different immigrant groups settled in different areas and created unique political communities. Daniel Elazar has suggested the existence of three distinct political cultures: Traditionalistic, Individualistic, and Moralistic. (Table 6-1 categorizes the states accordingly.) Embedded in a unique historical background and pattern of social development, each culture is distinguished by different beliefs about the purposes of government, the common good, and the proper boundaries of political activity. These cultural differences also suggest influences that affect electoral behavior.[7]

The Traditionalistic political culture (most commonly found in the Southern and Border states) sees government's primary purpose as the maintenance of order. Society is hierarchical, paternalistic, and preindustrial. Political competition is an elite preserve in which family and social ties predominate. Popular participation in political decision making is muted, if not actively discouraged. The politics is one-party dominant (Democratic). Competition is typified by elite factionalism or counter-elite insurgency. The overriding political goal is maintenance of the *status quo*.

[6] See Gabriel A. Almond and Sidney Verba, *The Civic Culture* (Boston: Little, Brown and Company, 1965).
[7] Ira Sharkansky, "The Utility of Elazar's Political Culture," *Polity* 2 (Fall 1969), 68.

Table 6-1   American States and Their Political Cultures

Moralistic	Individualistic	Traditionalistic
California	Alaska	Alabama
Colorado	Connecticut	Arizona
Idaho	Delaware	Arkansas
Iowa	Hawaii	Florida
Kansas	Illinois	Georgia
Maine	Indiana	Kentucky
Michigan	Maryland	Louisiana
Minnesota	Massachusetts	Mississippi
Montana	Nebraska	Missouri
New Hampshire	Nevada	New Mexico
North Dakota	New Jersey	North Carolina
Oregon	New York	Oklahoma
South Dakota	Ohio	South Carolina
Utah	Pennsylvania	Tennessee
Vermont	Rhode Island	Texas
Washington	Wyoming	Virginia
Wisconsin		West Virginia
Total = 17	Total = 16	Total = 17

Source: Adapted from Daniel J. Elazar, American Federalism: A View From The States (New York, Thomas Y. Crowell, 2nd ed., 1972), p. 118.

Mississippi is representative of the Traditionalistic culture. Essentially a closed and static society, the state is governed by a small elite who engage in factional quarrels. Political competition is typically "friends and neighbors" alliances struggling for control of the party organization; neither issues nor ideologies are important. This political order reflects the social system of the pre-Civil War plantation economy with minimal popular representation. In the post-Civil War era, the suffrage was restricted through devices such as the literacy test and the poll tax. This resulted in the disenfranchisement of the poor—White and Black alike. Government policy is custodial or reactionary. Regressive taxes, low social welfare payments, and anti-civil rights fillibusters are typical political activities. Ross Barnet (who as governor stood in the school house door to prevent integration) and James Eastland (the largest landowner in Sunflower County and a leading Senate conservative) are typical

Mississippi politicians, as were the reactionary Senators Vardaman and Bilbo.

The Individualistic political culture (mostly found in the Middle Atlantic, lower New England, and Great Lakes states) views the democratic order as analogous to the market place. This allows interests to compete freely, with government serving as referee. Government is laissez-faire, utilitarian, and essentially reactive. Public policy results from majority opinion, not a sense of justice. Parties exist to organize those interests, articulate their demands, and compete for power. Politics is essentially acquisitive—work for professionals. Its overriding goal is to maintain a balance among interests and between the public and private sectors.

Illinois, with a political organization like the Cook County Democratic Committee, typifies this culture. Trading the discretionary favors of government for political support, such organizations (machines) have mobilized large numbers of immigrant minorities into effective electoral coalitions. The operational norm is a *quid pro quo* of services for votes. Politics is transactional, and thus is popularly viewed as dirty, if not corrupt. Undeviating party regularity and organizational loyalty are the guiding principles. The worst evil is the primary fight, since it weakens the party in the general election and undermines the organizational reward structure. The machine is usually liberal on bread and butter issues that benefit its needy supporters. Its typical leaders—"Big Bill" Thompson, Anton Cermak, and Richard Daley—have been skilled technicians, able administrators, and consummate pragmatists.

The Moralistic political culture (found in upper New England, and in the North Central and Pacific states) sees government as a means for achieving a just social order and society's moral betterment. This political ethos emanates from those New England settlers bent on establishing a New Jerusalem. Politics is an instrument for the realization of private, as well as public, goals. The political style is egalitarian, amateur, nonpartisan (if often Republican), and in favor of good government. Political participation is a civic duty to be undertaken by all good citizens. The overriding political goal is improvement of the commonwealth—the use of political action to promote the public good.

Minnesota, with its citizen-politics tradition, illustrates this culture. Its politics is distinguished by an open caucus system of rank-and-file participation in Democratic-Farm-Labor Party affairs. Politics exists as a positive instrument for social good. Principles and issues are paramount, party and gain secondary; nonpartisan politics is often the rule. Public policy involves governmental intervention to promote communal equity (like utility and railroad regulation). Minnesota politicians like D-F-L founder Governor Floyd Olson, anti-Vietnam War leader Senator Eugene McCarthy, and civil rights advocate Senator Hubert Humphrey have stood for the Moralistic culture's politics.

The voting behaviors demonstrated in the different cultures are shown in Table 6-2. The Traditionalistic political culture

Table 6-2   Electoral Behavior: Variations with Political Culture

	Moralistic	Individualistic	Traditionalistic
Voted in 1970	68%	47%	66%
Did not vote in 1970	32%	53%	34%
Voted in all presidential elections	60%	35%	55%
Voted in some presidential elections	32%	48%	36%
Voted in no presidential elections	8%	17%	9%
Always voted for the same party for president	51%	48%	56%
Have voted for different parties for president	49%	52%	44%
Casts a straight ticket in local elections	37%	47%	62%
Casts a split ticket in local elections	63%	53%	38%

states reported the lowest level of voting in 1970 and the least regularity in presidential voting. Those with a Moralistic political culture reported the highest voting levels in 1970 and the greatest regularity in presidential voting. Individualistic states ranked between the other two types. In post-World War II gubernatorial and senatorial elections in non-presidential years, Moralistic culture Idaho had the highest average turnout. Traditionalistic culture Mississippi had the lowest by far of any state.[8]

These differences in electoral participation are not surprising. A Moralistic culture emphasizes political involvement as a civic responsibility and sees politics as a means for achieving community betterment. It is more likely to produce citizens with a positive belief in the value of voting. A Traditionalistic culture, emphasizing deference and the *status quo,* will have little popular participation, even where it has not been actively discouraged. An Individualistic culture, essentially pragmatic and pluralistic, will show moderate levels of participation.

The data in Table 6-2 also point to the influence of political culture on the individual's partisan consistency and degree of party regularity. Respondents in Individualistic states were the most likely to report voting for different parties in different elections. Respondents in Traditionalistic and Moralistic states were more consistent in their partisan choice. Within a given election, however, respondents from Moralistic states were the most likely to split their tickets by voting for candidates from different parties.

States influenced by the Traditionalistic political culture are dominated by one party—the Democratic. Individualistic states have competitive two-party systems while Moralistic states are two-party or modified one-party Republican (see Table 6-3). As would be expected in societies with highly professionalized politics, well-developed reward structures, and a multiplicity of

[8]Lester W. Milbrath, "Political Participation in the States," in *Politics in the American States: A Comparative Analysis,* 2nd ed., eds. Herbert Jacob and Kenneth Vines (Boston: Little, Brown and Company, 1971), 36.

Table 6-3   Degree of Party Competition and State Political Cultures

Moralistic		Individualistic		Traditionalistic	
California	2P	Alaska	2P	Alabama	1PD
Colorado	2P	Connecticut	2P	Arizona	2P
Idaho	2P	Delaware	2P	Arkansas	1PD
Iowa	2P	Hawaii	2P	Florida	MPD
Kansas	MPR	Illinois	2P	Georgia	1PD
Maine	2P	Indiana	2P	Kentucky	MPD
Michigan	2P	Maryland	MPD	Louisiana	1PD
Minnesota	2P	Massachusetts	2P	Mississippi	1PD
Montana	2P	Nebraska	2P	Missouri	MPD
New Hampshire	MPR	Nevada	2P	New Mexico	MPD
North Dakota	MPR	New Jersey	2P	North Carolina	MPD
Oregon	2P	New York	2P	Oklahoma	MPD
South Dakota	MPR	Ohio	2P	South Carolina	1PD
Utah	2P	Pennsylvania	2P	Tennessee	MPD
Vermont	MPR	Rhode Island	2P	Texas	1PD
Washington	2P	Wyoming	2P	Virginia	MPD
Wisconsin	2P			West Virginia	MPD

Classifications: 1PD = One-Party Democratic
MPD = Modified One-Party Democratic
2P = Two-Party (highly competitive parties)
MPR = Modified One-Party Republican

Source: Adapted from Austin Ranney, "Parties in State Politics" in Herbert Jacob and Kenneth N. Vines (eds.), Politics in American States: A Comparative Analysis 3rd ed., p. 85. Copyright © 1976, 1971, 1965 by Little, Brown and Company (Inc.) Reprinted by permission.

interest groups, politics in Individualistic states is competitive and partisan. While popular participation is lower than in Moralistic states, the intensity of inter-party rivalry is higher. The Moralistic states do not view politics in organizational terms or as a struggle between groups for access to power. Consequently, they have a weaker sense of partisanship and party competition. In the Traditionalistic states, competition takes place within the historically dominant party lest it endanger the stability of the prevailing social system. In the post-Reconstruction South, the ruling conservative elite argued that the Populist Party risked splitting the "white man's vote" and electing Republicans sympathetic to the recently freed slaves.

Respondents in Moralistic states reported the greatest political activity, as can be seen in Table 6-4. While political activity is generally low across the three cultures, people from Moralistic culture states were twice as likely as those from Traditionalistic states to attend political meetings, over twice as likely to be members of political organizations, and the most likely to try to influence others concerning electoral outcomes. Those from Individualistic states ranked consistently between the other two.

Table 6-4 Political Activity: Variation with Political Culture

		Moralistic	Individualistic	Traditionalistic
Try to Influence Anyone about Election	Yes	34%	25%	23%
	No	66%	75%	77%
Membership in Political Organization	Yes	8%	6%	3%
	No	92%	94%	97%
Attendance at Political Meetings	Yes	12%	10%	6%
	No	88%	90%	94%
Work for a Party or Candidate	Yes	10%	8%	4%
	No	90%	92%	96%
Display Campaign Literature	Yes	11%	9%	8%
	No	89%	91%	92%

The greater reported political activity in Moralistic states is consistent with that culture's perception of politics as a desirable endeavor. Every citizen is responsible for working to achieve the common good through positive action. It might also be reasonable to assume that people who perceive politics as a beneficial activity are not only more likely to participate but also to have a higher sense of political self-worth and generalized political awareness. The data in Table 6-5 support such an assumption.

Voters from Moralistic states were the most likely to disagree with statements that they had no political power and that

Table 6-5 Political Efficacy and Awareness: Variations with Political Culture.

	Moralistic	Individualistic	Traditionalistic
People like me have no political power.			
Agree	28%	35%	42%
Disagree	72%	65%	58%
Politics is too complicated for people like me.			
Agree	68%	72%	80%
Disagree	32%	28%	20%
Attention to Political Campaign			
Very Interested	36%	33%	32%
Somewhat Interested	44%	42%	43%
Not Much Interested	20%	25%	25%
Concern About Congressional Elections			
Very Much	29%	25%	25%
Pretty Much	45%	38%	38%
Not Much	26%	37%	37%

politics was too complicated to understand (although the vast majority of all resondents expressed a lack of political comprehension). This suggests a greater sense of political competence or efficacy. The Moralistic culture states also showed the most interest in political campaign activity and the greatest concern about electoral outcomes (although such interest was low in all states). Individualistic and Traditionalistic states ranked second and third respectively on these measures of political efficacy and awareness.

The historical and ethnocultural heritage that is the basis of a state's political culture provides the subjective orientation toward politics: the value system defining the context in which political behavior takes place.[9] Particularly in the Moralistic states, these values produce a citizenry that turns out to vote, is politically active, aware, highly efficacious, and concerned

[9] See the discussion of "Political Culture" by Sidney Verba in *The International Encyclopedia of the Social Sciences,* David L. Sills, ed. (New York: Macmillan, 1968).

about electoral outcomes—although basically indifferent to political parties. This combination of high political participation and intensity and low partisan effect is increasingly characteristic of the new politics so attractive to young, well-educated voters. It is also a development that is just starting to influence the style and content of American electoral politics.

THE INDEPENDENT ETHOS

Ethnocultural diversity can account for much of the wide variation in American political behavior. There are those who argue that past election results (especially in the nineteenth century) are understandable as clashes between two mutually exclusive religious world views: the pietistic and the ritualistic. The former, identified with New England evangelical Protestantism, favored temperance, abolitionism, nativism, public schools, and the Whig-Republican party. The latter, identified with nonevangelical Protestants (Lutheran, Dutch Reformed) and Catholic immigrants, resisted these efforts at the imposition of a moral hegemony through politics and supported the Democratic party. Lee Benson sees New York state voting behavior in the Jacksonian period as based on popular perceptions of the moral differences between the parties. Pious Yankees supported "Whig appeals for state-guided and state-enforced 'moral reformation.'" This was "precisely the kind of activist, collectivist state" most repugnant to the Dutch, whose moral viewpoint was not "as vivid and embracing as that held in New England."[10]

The Democrats became associated with political evangelism at the national level during the Bryan campaign of 1896.[11]

---

[10] Quoted in Richard L. McCormick, "Ethno-Cultural Interpretations of Nineteenth Century American Voting Behavior," *Political Science Quarterly* 89 (June 1974), 360.

[11] See Paul J. Kleppner, *The Cross of Culture: A Social Analysis of Mid-Western Politics, 1850–1900* (New York: The Free Press, 1970); and Richard J. Jensen, *The Winning of the Midwest: Social and Political Conflict, 1888–1896* (Chicago: University of Chicago Press, 1971).

Nevertheless, the strength of conscience Republicanism is evidenced by its dominance in the Moralistic culture states. The politics of state sponsored morality—personal and official—is very much alive where the Yankee heritage is still strong. The Individualistic culture states are not only more heterogeneous, but they are also inhabited by an immigrant population with religious views less regulative of public behavior. Tolerance, not temperance, is the required virtue if politics is to function as usual.

The Yankee political culture has also been identified as a good government or public regarding ethos as opposed to the immigrant culture based on personal loyalties and private-regardingness.[12] The institutional expressions of the Yankee culture were nonpartisanship, the city manager, and impartial enforcement of the laws. The Immigrant culture expressed itself in the machine, the boss, and discretionary treatment. People who support universalistic and community-serving conceptions of the public good are more likely to be Yankee or Jewish, and to be better educated and more affluent. Those who support localistic and people-serving concepts are more likely to be Catholic, with relatively low incomes and little schooling.

What this suggests is a class dimension to differences in political culture. The Moralistic-Yankee culture is that of middle-class professionals who also hold an Independent political ethos. This highly educated class is more issue conscious than other voters and more likely to vote on the basis of a candidate's appeal than on the basis of party affiliation. Such voters are not only the most likely to split their tickets and swing between parties; but they are also the least likely to identify with a party at all. These new Independents come disproportionately from the young, college-educated, high income, professional-managerial strata.

Among the under thirty-five age group, more people identify themselves as Independents than as either Democrats or Repub-

[12] James Q. Wilson and Edward C. Banfield, "Public Regardingness as a Value Premise in Voting Behavior," *American Political Science Review* 58 (December 1964), 876-87.

licans. More important, these Independents are an extremely influential group: vocal, articulate, skilled, politically active, self-assured. These Independents suggest the development of a new political culture, national rather than regional in scope, with increasing consequences for candidate selection and election results. Like the Moralistic culture, this new politics is political but antiparty, participatory but antiorganizational, more concerned with moral than economic betterment, reformist but not radical, progressive but not populist, and more concerned with means to the exclusion of ends, and with the appearance of things rather than their meaning.

The public has become enamored of nonpolitical, or, more accurately, transpolitical, candidates who seek to purify government. Representatives of this political strain have been elected on planks that have questioned the conventional mode of governmental operations: Brown in California, Walker in Illinois, Lamm in Colorado, Dukakis in Massachusetts. As governors, they have operated without ideological consistency and have articulated a concern that Americans change their values and material life style. While liberal on most issues, these new politicians also advocate social austerity and fiscal conservatism.

This new politics, like nineteenth century Mugwumpism, involves a commitment to procedural, rather than substantive, reform that is very appealing to well-educated professionals. It is the contemporary manifestation of a recurring political impulse that has championed "good government" and "principle above politics." The recent Presidential campaigns of Senators McCarthy and McGovern (and also that of Senator Goldwater) were characterized as "pursuing moral goals through politics, motivated by civic spirit, without any desire for personal gain, concerned with raising the right issues and in creating the right climate in which the issue might be considered."[13] Unfortunately, it is possible to be neither right nor

[13] Daniel J. Elazar, *American Federalism: A View From the States,* 2nd ed. (New York: Thomas Y. Crowell, 1972), 137–39.

president, especially if the political ethos is considered antagonistic to prevailing values and indifferent to popular needs. New politics does not necessarily make for good government if its morality is perceived as self-righteous and hypocritical.

IMPLICATIONS

Too often in politics we become fixed on the current problem and the surface activity. Newspaper headlines—those flowers that fade before grasped twice—can blind us to underlying dimensions and broader themes. Political values are such phenomena. Indeed, much policy-making reflects long standing value commitments, not themselves the subject of political debate. Values are the enduring backdrop against which daily crises take place. Fundamental political change is thus glacial despite the ins and outs of election results.

Political strategy must take into account a state's heritage and adapt its style accordingly. Electoral appeals should be tailored to meet popular preconceptions about appropriate goals. Programs should be constructed to conform to tradition-sanctioned procedures. A program's substance is not altered simply by proclaiming it the continuation of existing commitments. Political change is difficult under the most ideal conditions; many a worthy reform has failed because tradition was unnecessarily flouted. Successful reforms are those that promise to alleviate problems while not seeming to threaten traditional values.

The slowness of political change reflects society's essentially organic nature. Unlike an automobile, a political system does not respond automatically or predictably to changes in velocity. There is all the difference between willing a particular policy outcome and its realization. Politics is the essential linkage between policy intent and program performance. Not only is policy success related to political problematics, it is not completely predictable. Purposive action often has completely unanticipated consequences. Two examples should illustrate this.

The personal registration requirement for voting was introduced in order to end corrupt election practices like plural voting and personation. Reflecting middle-class values, the burden of compliance was placed on the individual—who was expected to be familiar with the legal technicalities, registration deadlines, and location of the board of elections. Consequently, many a peripatetic professional has been unwittingly disenfranchised. The disenfranchisement of the poor is more dramatic. Whether or not the resulting electorate is better, it is smaller and unrepresentative. Similarly, the reforms introduced by the Federal Campaign Act of 1974 limiting campaign spending may result in major electoral distortions. Both the Conservative Party of New York and the New York Civil Liberties Union (hardly ideological bedmates) have argued that the spending limits violate freedom of speech, favor incumbents, and discriminate against independent candidates.[14]

There is no faulting the good intentions of these reforms. Nevertheless, the consequences are not beyond question even by their original supporters. Good intentions can pave the road to more than one undesirable location. Similarly, crusades to reform society can degenerate into platitudes and meaningless slogans. More than one Noble Experiment to abolish an undesirable state of affairs has created outcomes worse than the original problem.

These observations are rather pointedly directed at the Moralistic political culture. This would be a bit unfair were its values not too often accepted uncritically by young voters. Practical politics is often at odds with uncompromising principle. High hopes usually prove disappointing when placed against the enormity of social problems. Achieving success is more difficult than stating the problem. Some warning may prevent these disappointments from resulting in a self-defeating

---

[14]David Adamany and George Agree, "Election Campaign Financing: The 1974 Reforms," *Political Science Quarterly* 90 (Summer 1975), 219.

and self-indulgent cynicism. Many aspects of a Moralistic political culture are highly recommendable: a politically active and highly efficacious electorate, aware of issues and electorally selective. Nevertheless, its indifference to the legitimate role of parties in the political process and to the importance of ends as well as means deprives elections of policy coherence and the electorate of meaningful choice.

CHAPTER SEVEN

The Future of Voting

This discussion has analyzed the varieties of voting in America: national, subnational, primaries. The focus has been on the main components of elections: turnout patterns, party loyalty, party competition, issue awareness, political culture. What conclusions can we draw? What speculations can we venture?

CONCLUSIONS

The principle conclusion must be one that stresses differences: differences between the actual and potential electorates; differences between the electorates and their behaviors in presidential and non-presidential elections; differences among states and differences between the electorate today and that of a generation ago. If elections have any importance in the American political process, then these differences are of more than academic interest. They raise questions about which groups receive government benefits, about what types of politicians will achieve public office, and about what they will do once elected.

Not everyone who is legally entitled to vote exercises the

franchise. Compared to parliamentary elections in most democratic countries, turnout in American presidential elections is embarrassingly low. As we move from presidential elections to off-year Congressional elections, and from state elections in the odd-numbered years to primary elections or to elections held at times other than the traditional date in November, turnout plummets. These differences may result from institutional factors such as voter registration and the timing of elections. (Most other countries do not require personal registration and hold their elections on weekends in the spring or fall.) Cultural differences between the United States and the older societies of Europe, and the lesser importance of non-presidential elections, also contribute. Nevertheless, the differences remain politically important because of the differential turnout rates of various social groups. Basically, the lower the turnout in an election, the greater will be the overrepresentation of Whites instead of Blacks, the middle class instead of the working class, the educated instead of the uneducated. Primary elections are particularly middle class. Since high turnout groups have interests that are distinct from (if not antithetical to) those of low turnout groups, the result may be a significant bias in government policy. The greater frequency of elections hurts the poor, who lack the resources to keep informed about the candidates and issues involved. Low turnout gives an edge to the forces best organized to muster voters to the polls. The turnout—its size and composition—can determine who wins.

In the 1950s, American voters overwhelmingly thought of themselves as partisans: either Democrats or Republicans. This subjective sense of party identification was the strongest influence on electoral behavior. Not only was there a high correlation between partisanship and vote; issue opinions and other politically relevant attitudes were also strongly conditioned by partisanship. Since the 1950s, a number of important changes have occurred, especially the dramatic decline in the overall level of partisanship. Party identification remains a powerful predictor of vote for those who have an identification, but more and more voters lack one. Older voters, brought up in an earlier and more partisan era, are being replaced by the independent young. Since those who enter the electorate as Independents will likely remain so, the overall importance of party identification will dramatically decline.

The Democrats are the predominant party in the South and Northeast; they are the party of the Black, of the working class, of the Catholic and Jew. Over the last two decades, however, Democratic strength in the South has been eroded, while its strength in the Northeast has increased. Class and religious differences are less important; but the racial difference has become larger: A vastly higher proportion of Blacks consider themselves Democrats than was true twenty years ago. In both presidential and non-presidential elections, Republicans are more likely to vote than Democrats, and the partisans of either party are more likely to vote than Independents. The differences are especially great in the less salient off-year elections. The correlation between partisanship and vote was the highest in Congressional elections.

While partisanship has been declining in importance, the significance of issues has increased. Compared to the 1950s, more people have more opinions about more issues, are more likely to have an idea about where the parties stand on the issues, and are more likely to vote in ways consistent with their issue opinions. All of these trends are most pronounced in the off-year elections. People were more willing to attribute policy positions to the parties in 1970 than in 1972. These evaluations were also more likely to be consistent with partisan preference. The social and political problems that surfaced in the 1960s enhanced the significance of issues. The 1960s produced a new breed of Independents, more issue oriented politicians, and a new politics generally. Whether such a policy-directed style of politics will persist remains to be seen. In the past, politicians overestimated partisan loyalties and ignored the voters' policy demands. The parties have paid a heavy price for their failure to take issues seriously.

As party competition increases, voter turnout is higher. So are attendance at political meetings, campaign activity, organizational membership, and feelings of subjective political competence. Competitive states have a greater sense of political power and lower levels of political cynicism and ignorance than less competitive states. On the other hand, citizens in competitive states are less likely to view voting as an effective political weapon. It would seem that electors in non-competitive states have had more experience with consistently voting for winners. Hence they are more likely to perceive voting as a potent political force.

American states and the politics of their citizenry can also be differentiated according to their value systems. Political culture is the summary name applied to these politically relevant attitudes and beliefs. Traditionalistic states are characterized by lower voter turnout, low party competition, little political involvement, and low levels of political efficacy. Individualistic states have medium turnout levels, strong inter-party competition, and moderate levels of political activity and awareness. Moralistic states have the highest turnout rates, medium party competitiveness, and the highest levels of activity and awareness.

These conclusions present three voting paradoxes that are at odds with normal theoretical expectations. The first notion contrary to conventional wisdom is the Paradox of Participation. A good turnout should be representative of the population as a whole, yet such an electorate is badly informed and politically immature. On the other hand, this electorate is moderate while the well-informed citizens who vote in non-presidential elections are both more partisan and more ideologically extreme. The swing in electoral returns comes from the least-informed and least-committed voters.

The Paradox of Democracy involves the contradiction between popular control over individual politicians and control over the policy-making process. Maximizing the first impedes the second. When the voters may hold politicians individually accountable in frequent general elections and in regular primaries, party cohesion is undermined. Politicians must bend to pressures from individual constituents as well as to the dominant party factions and interest groups. Consequently, wide differences open between the policy views of politicians within the same party. As ever greater numbers of officials are directly elected, and as primaries become increasingly prevalent, the importance of this trend grows. Yet as more officials are elected, voters are forced to rely on partisanship as a voting cue. If voters cannot hold all the candidates of the party in power accountable for government policy, their ability to control that policy through electoral rewards and punishments vanishes.

The Paradox of Reform refers to the experience of good intentions having bad results. Procedural reforms like the Australian ballot and personal registration contributed to declining party voting and overall turnout. The primary, more blatantly anti-party, lessened the responsiveness of parties to popular needs and encouraged intra-party factionalism and ideological extremism. Slogans like "vote for the person, not the party" create an illusion of principle over politics when the reality is ignorance of candidates and principleless politics. Despite the counter-productivity of many of these reforms, they represent deeply held upper middle-class value commitments. These are not to be lightly regarded; there is no wrath like that of the upper middle class when its values have been scorned.

SPECULATIONS

A theme that has recurred throughout this analysis is the electorate's increasing independence. From 1940 to 1965, Independents constituted between 20 and 22% of the electorate. A 1975 Gallup poll reported that 22% of the voters saw themselves as Republicans, 46% as Democrats, and 32% as Independents. Among voters under thirty, Independents outnumber Democratic and Republican identifiers combined.[1]

[1]Samuel P. Huntington, "The Democratic Distemper," *The Public Interest* 41 (Fall 1975), 20.

Independence is not an option in the voting booth where choices must be made among party nominees. Nevertheless, the public's attitudes and inconsistent voting patterns fairly shout "A plague on both your houses."

The rise in independence (or decline in partisanship) is a post-1964 phenomenon. Before then, the distribution of partisan attachments was remarkably stable. Public dissatisfaction with the parties can be explained by their poor performance on the issues that have rent American society in the past decade. Many Democrats-turned-Independents are segregationist Southerners displeased with their party's racial tolerance; others are Catholics displeased with the party's position on social issues (like the "amnesty, abortion, and acid" stands attributed to George McGovern); still others were repelled by the Johnson administration's war policies. The Republicans-turned-Independents are largely middle-class Protestant, well-educated, Northern suburbanites displeased with the Goldwater candidacy, the Nixon Southern strategy, Agnew appeals for law and order, and Watergate.[2]

The former Democrats and former Republicans constitute a growing body of unaligned, atomized voters. More important is the absence of party attachment among the youngest voters. Those aged twenty to twenty-nine are twice as likely to be Independents as those over fifty. The new voters are the most affected by the recent political turmoil—especially Vietnam—and are clearly reluctant to form any political allegiances at all. For the best-educated, most-affluent, highest-mobility generation, the parties have little importance as reference points.

Current voting behavior strongly suggests an underlying alienation and decline in electoral conscientiousness. The configuration of the new electorate is familiar: At the subnational level the voters are unrepresentative of either the general electorate or general population, better-informed but hostile to parties; and the national electorate is larger and more like the

---

[2]This discussion is based on James L. Sundquist, "Whither the American Party System," *Political Science Quarterly* 88 (December 1973), 571-79.

general population, but ill-informed and unreliable. Independence, ticket splitting, high partisan swings, and candidate selectivity are the rule—especially for those voters most likely to vote often. The new electorate and new politics—reputedly more enlightened than the old—may prove the nemesis of the electoral process, not its salvation.

The New Politics aims to reform American society not simply by reforming institutions but by achieving a reformation of its basic values. Whether such an overt politicization of the moral realm is desirable is debatable; even more debatable is the use of electoral politics to achieve that end. Moralistic political campaigns are usually too diffuse and speculative to stand up under analysis. What they have in promissory visions they usually lack in precise political plans; what they offer in heightened expectations, they lack in realistic governmental programs. The practical problems of translating ideas into results cannot be cavalierly dismissed as trivial or technical. New programs need to be evaluated for the increment of social good offered, the availability of resources to achieve the goal, the likelihood of success, and the possible unintended consequences.

If politics is the nexus between ideas and policy, analysis is the link between political goals and programmatic success. Much of the political program of the new politics consists of miscellaneous platitudes bereft of policy analysis or program evaluation. Some detailed criteria for making public choices must be established before moral reformation can begin. Public policy analysis, like the rules of grammar, is a necessary first-order undertaking—however tiresome such exercises may be. Like many moral crusades, the new politics is long on faith and short on doctrine.

Supporters of the new politics seek magic procedural reforms that will render the political order more positive and respectable. Attacking the parties, however, has resulted in less, not more, popular control. With the parties debilitated, the voters are deprived of the symbols, cues, and vehicles necessary for mass participation. Deprived of organizational vitality and popular support, the parties are increasingly less able to weld economic, geographic, and ethnic fractions into electoral coalitions.

American parties have often been criticized for their ideological incoherence and office orientation. On the other hand, this stance has minimized fractious debates and contributed to the stability of American politics. Conflict takes place over the distribution of material rewards (matters that can be settled by the techniques of bargaining, compromise, and mutual adjustment of differences), rather than points of principle (matters that often lead to value-conflict, forced choices, and the polarization of public opinion). By minimizing ideological conflict, American parties have accommodated divers (and diverse) elements that might otherwise form their own parties. Such a multi-party system would probably include socialist, Northern conservative, Southern conservative, Southern populist, and country parties, as well as ethnocultural parties based on race, linguistics, or religion.[3] The specter of this political Balkanization argues against too thorough an ideological overhaul of the American party system.

The government has assumed the social welfare role once played by the parties. The primary has stripped the parties of control over who will carry their labels. Political consulting firms package candidates and sell them directly to the public, bypassing the parties. The public lacks confidence in the ability of the parties to guarantee responsive government. These gloomy assessments of the party system's condition have produced speculation about a major party realignment or third party movement.[4]

One conjecture has the Democrats combining upper middle-class technocrats and the Black underclass against the Republi-

---

[3]Seymour Martin Lipset, "The Paradox of American Politics," *The Public Interest* 41 (Fall 1975), 156.

[4]Arthur H. Miller, "Political Issues and Trust in Government: 1964-1970," *American Political Science Review* 68 (September 1974), 971.

can Middle America and White working class. Alternatively, the parties could simply disappear—since they no longer broker interests, control the economic system, or integrate people into the political community.[5] The parties would be replaced by a wide variety of *ad hoc* special purpose groups, personal campaign organizations, and political branches of trade associations and the labor unions.

Despite the parties' poor condition, it is premature to file their obituaries. They are very much alive and likely to get livelier. As American politics moves away from its concern with moral theology to confront economic issues, party politics becomes relevant once again. Not that the old style bosses and machines will be rescued from the political ash heap; they are technologically (and sociologically) obsolete. Nevertheless, the new politics of the 1970s and 1980s has rediscovered traditional economic concerns; Amnesty, Acid, and Abortion have given way to Austerity, Inflation, and Unemployment.

These problems of fiscal policy, economic planning, and social welfare are the stock-in-trade of both parties. They offer an opportunity for the Democrats to reconstruct their New Deal coalition (urban, union, immigrant) against the Middle American Republican forces (suburban and rural, professional, native born). The real challenge facing the American parties is to restore public confidence in elections as a means of controlling government and directing public policy. The future of voting in America depends upon how successfully the parties respond to popular hopes and upon how faithfully they fulfill their promises.

---

[5]See Walter Dean Burnham, *Critical Elections and the Mainsprings of American Politics* (New York: W. W. Norton, 1970).